MARGARET
POLE

MARGARET POLE

POLE

THE COUNTESS IN THE TOWER

SUSAN HIGGINBOTHAM

AMBERLEY

First published 2016

Amberley Publishing
The Hill, Stroud
Gloucestershire, GL5 4EP

www.amberley-books.com

Copyright © Susan Higginbotham, 2016

The right of Susan Higginbotham to be
identified as the Author of this work has been
asserted in accordance with the Copyrights,
Designs and Patents Act 1988.

ISBN 978 1 4456 3594 1 (hardback)
ISBN 978 1 4456 3609 2 (ebook)

British Library Cataloguing in Publication Data.
A catalogue record for this book is available
from the British Library.

Typesetting and Origination by Amberley
Publishing.
Printed in the UK.

CONTENTS

AUTHOR'S NOTE

For consistency's sake and ease of reading, in quoting from contemporary sources I have used modern spelling whenever possible. Names are generally given the spelling used by the *Oxford Dictionary of National Biography*.

I

DAUGHTER OF VIOLENCE

On 27 May 1541, the denizens of the Tower of London witnessed a scene that shocked even the hardiest of execution-goers: a noblewoman of sixty-seven, a venerable age at the time, was led to a block and ordered to lay down her head. There, a 'wretched and blundering youth', inexperienced at his grisly task, ended the life of Margaret Pole, Countess of Salisbury, 'hack[ing] her head and shoulders to pieces in the most pitiful manner'.

It was a shocking end – and yet not an entirely unfitting one. For from her earliest years, violence had stalked Margaret.

* * *

Margaret's story begins in the struggle for the throne between the houses of York and Lancaster known today as the Wars of the Roses. In 1461, Edward, Earl of March, son of the late Richard, Duke of York, had seized the throne from the politically inept and mentally unstable Lancastrian king, Henry VI. His greatest ally had been Richard Neville, Earl of Warwick, a rich and powerful lord whose efforts on Edward's behalf led later writers to dub him the 'Kingmaker'.

Not quite nineteen, Edward was unmarried when he took the throne, a situation he remedied – shockingly – in 1464. His bride, whom he married secretly, was not the expected foreign, virgin princess but one of his subjects, Elizabeth Woodville, a widow with two children. Her husband, Sir John Grey, had fallen while fighting for the house of Lancaster. Edward's new queen had no wealth to speak of, but did have a large family. Their growing influence at court and disputes over foreign policy soon alienated Warwick from the young man he had assisted to the throne.

There was no shortage of sore spots between Warwick and Edward IV, but one in particular is germane here. Warwick and his countess, the heiress Anne Beauchamp, had failed to produce any surviving sons, but did have two daughters, Isabel and Anne. Edward IV had two younger brothers – George, Duke of Clarence, and Richard, Duke of Gloucester – whose ages and circumstances made them perfect matches for Warwick's daughters. Unfortunately, while Warwick saw this quite clearly, the king did not. Undeterred, Warwick secretly procured a papal dispensation for George (born 21 October 1449) and Isabel (born 5 September 1451) to marry. The wedding, performed by the Archbishop of York (it helped that he was George Neville, Warwick's younger brother), followed on 11 July 1469 at Calais. The wedding festivities were not prolonged, for Warwick and his new son-in-law and ally immediately launched a rebellion against the king, whom the pair held captive for a short time. The rebellion soon fizzled out, but not before Warwick and Clarence had executed Elizabeth Woodville's father and one of her brothers and killed some other upstarts as well.

No one expected the ensuing rapprochement between the king and the rebels to last long, and it did not. The situation rapidly deteriorated until the spring of 1470, when Warwick and Clarence took ship to Calais. With them came the Countess of Warwick, her younger daughter, Anne, and the heavily pregnant Isabel, Duchess of Clarence. It was while aboard ship that Isabel gave birth to her and Clarence's child, who was so short-lived that John Rous, who lovingly recorded the genealogy of the earls of Warwick, did not know his or her gender. The unfortunate babe was buried at sea.[1]

Having spent some years in exile and as a fugitive since losing his throne, the hapless Henry VI had been captured in 1465 and confined to the Tower. His queen, Margaret of Anjou, had fled to her native France, where she had been living in an impoverished exile that increasingly looked permanent. Warwick's rebellion transformed this. With the encouragement of King Louis XI of France, Warwick entered into an alliance with Margaret, sealing the deal by marrying his younger daughter, Anne, to Henry and Margaret's only child, Edward of Lancaster. In the autumn of 1470, Warwick succeeded in driving Edward out of England and restoring Henry VI to the throne.

Edward IV was not one to leave his throne quietly. In exile, he devoted himself to raising his own army, with which he returned to England. In April 1471, his forces met Warwick's at Barnet. There Warwick was killed. Before the battle, Warwick had been deserted by Clarence, who had given in to family pressure and reconciled with his brother Edward.

The next month Edward scored a second Yorkist victory, this time at Tewkesbury, where Henry VI's son Edward, fighting his first battle, was killed. Margaret of Anjou was taken as a prisoner to the Tower. Hours after her arrival, Henry VI, who himself had been imprisoned in the Tower after the Battle of Barnet, died, probably on Edward's orders.

With Edward IV back on the throne, he and his brothers turned to the business of seeing to the vast estates of Warwick and his countess, on which both Clarence and his younger brother Gloucester cast a covetous eye. Edward of Lancaster's death at Tewkesbury had left Anne Neville a young widow, a situation soon remedied by Gloucester. In a highly irregular action, Parliament declared the Countess of Warwick legally dead, enabling Clarence and Gloucester to lay claim to her lands in the Midlands and the north through their wives, although it would take several years for them to be divided to the brothers' satisfaction.

It was against this backdrop that Isabel, Duchess of Clarence, gave birth to Margaret on 14 August 1473 at Farleigh Castle. Three years before, she had given birth aboard ship while fleeing with her parents and husband into an uncertain future. This time, whatever pains Isabel suffered in bringing her daughter into the world, she could take comfort in the fact that she was labouring in the comfort of her own bedchamber, properly attended and enjoying all of the luxuries of a ducal household. As England was at peace, Isabel could have also hoped with all confidence that her infant daughter – assuming she did not fall prey to illness – would have a conventional future before her, which for a girl of her rank meant marriage to another member of the nobility, preferably one well endowed with land.

Margaret was named not for the imprisoned and defeated Margaret of Anjou but most likely for her aunt Margaret, Duchess of Burgundy. The duchess had been absent from England since her marriage to Charles, Duke of Burgundy, in 1468, but she reportedly regarded Clarence as her favourite brother.[2] It may be that she served as Margaret's godmother by proxy.

Little is known of Margaret's earliest years, but they certainly would have been comfortable ones. In December 1468, Clarence, then only nineteen, drew up an ordinance specifying the organization of his enormous household. His 'riding household' – those who travelled with him from estate to estate – comprised 188 persons. Clarence's marriage in 1469 to Isabel swelled the household further: the duchess had her own entourage, which included a baroness, five gentlewomen, a yeoman waferer and a yeoman of her horses.[3]

At the time the ordinances were drafted the duke and duchess were childless, but Margaret would have soon acquired her own small entourage. Most likely Isabel would have had a wet nurse for her daughter, and probably a 'rocker' to keep the infant's cradle in motion. A mistress of the nursery would probably be engaged to oversee these servants, particularly when, on 25 February 1475, Isabel bore a son, Edward, Earl of Warwick, necessitating an enlargement of the nursery staff. As his father's heir, young Warwick would have eclipsed his sister in importance from the day he drew breath.

A year later, young Margaret's world began to unravel. On 6 October 1476, Isabel bore another son, Richard. Perhaps due to complications from childbirth, she died just two months afterward, on 22 December 1476, at twenty-five. Richard followed his mother to the grave on 1 January 1477.[4] This was a sad state of affairs, but not an unusual one, as many women died of complications related to childbirth and many children died in infancy. How deeply her mother's death affected Margaret we cannot say; noblewomen generally left the day-to-day care of their young children to others, often travelling between their estates and to court while the children stayed at a fixed location. Whatever the emotional impact of Isabel's death upon Margaret, her position as a duke's daughter, surrounded by servants, meant that her day-to-day life would have gone on much as it had when her mother was still alive. The next change for Margaret, however, would be cataclysmic.

For a short period, it appeared that Margaret would gain a stepmother, either the very rich Mary of Burgundy or a sister of James III of Scotland. Edward IV, however, thwarted both matches. This did nothing to improve his relationship with Clarence, which since the brothers' reconciliation in 1471 seems to have been rather formal. From here, things went swiftly downhill. In April 1477 Clarence had his men seize Ankarette Twynho, one of the Duchess of Clarence's servants, and accused the hapless woman of poisoning her mistress on 10 October 1476 – more than two months before the unfortunate duchess actually died. For good measure, Clarence accused John Thursby of poisoning the duke's infant son, Richard, with ale administered on 21 December 1476. Ankarette and John were hauled to Clarence's stronghold of Warwick Castle, where after a trial by a cowed jury they were executed despite the improbability of the charges.

Meanwhile, a member of Clarence's household, Thomas Burdett, was having his own troubles: he and an astronomer named John Stacy were accused of using astronomy to predict the deaths of the king and his eldest son – an act of treason for which the men paid with their lives in May 1477. When Clarence came to Burdett's defence shortly thereafter by having a friar read his protestations of innocence to the king's council, this proved too much for Edward IV. In June 1477, Clarence was imprisoned in the Tower. On 18 February 1478, he was executed. Supposedly he was drowned in a barrel of malmsey wine or, less picturesquely, in a bathtub made of the barrels used to hold such wine. Notably, in the portrait supposed to be of Margaret, she wears a bracelet with a little barrel on her right wrist – though whether this confirms the veracity of the legend or simply echoes the legend itself cannot be said.

Margaret and her younger brother, Edward, were now the children of an attainted traitor. This was not necessarily fatal to their prospects, as attainders could be and often were reversed after a decent interval to allow a child to inherit his father's property, and Margaret as the king's niece remained an attractive marital prospect. Still, Margaret's status had abruptly changed from that of a duke's daughter to a dependent orphan niece, and she must have grieved for her parents as well to at least some extent.

Following Clarence's execution, Margaret's brother Edward, Earl of Warwick, became a ward of the Crown. Wardships in the fifteenth century were lucrative commodities, allowing the guardian to profit from the ward's estates and often to arrange his marriage as well, and as such the king would grant or sell them to favoured courtiers. In September 1480, in exchange for £2,000, Edward IV granted young Warwick's wardship to his stepson Thomas Grey, Marquis of Dorset.[5] The eldest of Elizabeth Woodville's two sons from her first marriage, Dorset had a large and growing family, and most likely intended to marry the young earl to one of his many daughters. Probably Warwick was raised on one of Dorset's estates in the country.

Where Margaret spent this time is unrecorded. She may have stayed in the company of her brother for a time, but it seems more likely that she was raised in the royal household with the king and queen's bevy of daughters. Certainly she was properly clothed and attended: in January 1482, Edward IV ordered the Exchequer to pay 40 marks for her clothing and the wages of her servants. He ordered another payment, this time of 50 marks, the following November.[6]

But Margaret would soon find herself under the care of a new uncle: Richard, Duke of Gloucester, Edward IV's only surviving brother following Clarence's execution. Edward IV's sudden death in April 1483 left his twelve-year-old son, Edward V, as the new King of England. Claiming that the queen's family was plotting against him, Gloucester imprisoned Elizabeth's brother, Anthony, Earl Rivers, and her second son by her first marriage, Richard Grey, and took the rule of the country into his hands as Edward V's protector. Elizabeth hastened into sanctuary at Westminster Abbey, where she remained with her daughters until 1484.

After some weeks of governing as his nephew's protector, Gloucester discovered or pretended to discover (opinions vary) that before his marriage to Elizabeth Woodville, Edward IV had been married to one Eleanor Talbot, thereby rendering his marriage to Elizabeth invalid and Edward V and his siblings illegitimate. Having made this revelation public, and having discouraged any opposition by sending for an army from the north and by executing his erstwhile ally William, Lord Hastings, without trial, Gloucester took the throne as Richard III. One of his last acts as protector had been to order the executions of Anthony Woodville and Richard Grey.

There were two more obstacles to Richard's taking the throne, however: Warwick and young Margaret, his nephew and niece. Were the line of succession strictly followed, Warwick, as the son of Clarence, should have been king once Edward IV's children were disqualified. Richard, however, claimed that due to Clarence's attainder, his children were barred from taking the throne.[7] In fact, as Hazel Pierce points out, the attainder did not mention the claims of Clarence's children,[8] and in any case Parliament could have obligingly reversed the attainder if Warwick were put on the throne. But as mere children, Warwick and Margaret were not in a position to press their claims, nor did they attract any supporters in a country that was already reeling from the ease with which Gloucester had assumed the throne.

Shortly after becoming Edward V's protector, the Duke of Gloucester had ordered that Warwick be brought from the country to the household of his wife, Anne, Warwick's maternal aunt.[9] When Gloucester was crowned as Richard III on 6 July, Warwick was among those present.[10] His treatment contrasts with that of Edward IV's sons, Edward V and his brother Richard, Duke of York. Having been lodged at the Tower of London in anticipation of Edward V's never-to-be-held coronation, they were seen less and less often within its precincts until they finally vanished altogether.[11] Their fate remains a mystery, but on balance it seems likely that Richard, fearing a rising on their behalf, had them killed.

Warwick, however, neither died nor disappeared. Rather, when Richard III went on a royal progress to the north soon after his coronation, young Warwick was in his train. He was an honoured member of it, for at York on 8 September 1483, Richard invested his own young son as Prince of Wales and knighted Warwick.[12] Why was Warwick treated differently from his royal cousins? As his legitimacy had not been questioned, he had a claim to the throne that was better than Richard's, and Richard could not be certain that no one would remember this. Perhaps, to borrow from Oscar Wilde, to lose two nephews might be regarded as a misfortune; to lose three might be deemed carelessness. Most likely, however, Richard's careful treatment of young Warwick was motivated by pragmatism. The previous holder of the earldom of Warwick, Richard's late father-in-law Richard Neville, had been a powerful figure in the north, and upon entering the lands in the 1470s Richard had succeeded in winning the northerners' respect and loyalty. Allowing any harm to come to young Warwick, Richard Neville's grandson, would have alienated Richard's most dependable supporters. Furthermore, unlike Edward IV's sons, whose supporters tried to free them from the Tower just weeks after Richard's coronation, no one seemed inclined to rise on behalf of Warwick. Probably Richard was taking a wait-and-see attitude toward his third nephew, and was prepared to treat him well if no trouble arose on his behalf. No doubt the fact that

Warwick was the son of his queen's only legitimate sister was a consideration for Richard as well.

Margaret probably accompanied her brother north in 1483 and remained there with him. By 8 June 1484, she and her brother were both ensconced at one of the king's northern estates, probably Sandal Castle. On that date, Richard ordered that fine materials – including cloth of gold, velvet, satin and damask – be purchased for Warwick and Margaret, as well as for Katherine, Richard's illegitimate daughter, and her future husband, William Herbert, Earl of Huntingdon. Probably these expensive fabrics were purchased in preparation for a special occasion, such as the wedding of Katherine and Huntingdon.[13] This order, discovered only recently, offers a rare glimpse of Margaret during Richard's reign. Not quite eleven in June 1484, she was reaching an age where her marriage would have been of interest to her uncle.

Richard III's reign had not gone smoothly. Just weeks after his coronation, there had been an attempt to free Edward V from the Tower. Rumours of the princes' death, never denied by Richard III, soon led to yet another uprising in the autumn of 1483 with the intention of bringing an exiled nobleman, Henry Tudor, to the throne.

Henry Tudor was the son of Edmund Tudor, Earl of Richmond, a younger half-brother of Henry VI. Edmund had married a very young heiress, Margaret Beaufort, and promptly consummated the marriage. His death left Margaret a pregnant widow at the age of only thirteen. Although Margaret would marry two more times, she would have no more children; nonetheless, the single son she did bear in January 1457 would give his name to a new dynasty.

In 1483, however, Henry Tudor seemed the unlikeliest of kings. In 1462, he had been made the ward of William, Lord Herbert, who was killed in battle in 1469. He ended up in the care of his paternal uncle, Jasper Tudor, who opposed Edward IV in the tumultuous years of 1470–71. In September 1471, Jasper and Henry had escaped to Brittany and had remained there ever since. With no experience running his own estates, much less a nation, and no experience in battle, he was not the most promising of kingly candidates – yet the rebels, many of whom had served Edward IV, were willing to take the chance.

The rebellion (known as Buckingham's rebellion for its highest-ranking conspirator, Henry Stafford, Duke of Buckingham) failed, leaving Henry Tudor, who had sailed for England but prudently declined to disembark when he sensed that a trap lay ashore, to return to exile. Nonetheless, on Christmas Day 1483 he and his fellow exiles came together at Rennes Cathedral, where Henry vowed to marry Edward IV's eldest daughter, Elizabeth of York, who at the time was still in sanctuary with her mother and sisters.

Although Richard III could congratulate himself on having put down the uprising so satisfactorily, the ensuing months gave him little other cause for cheer. In the spring of 1484, his only legitimate son died; in March 1485, his queen died. Rumours soon circulated that Richard was planning to marry his niece, Elizabeth of York, who had recently come out of sanctuary and who had been welcomed at court. Publicly denying the rumours, Richard determined to stop the wagging tongues by sending Elizabeth north, where she probably joined her cousins Warwick and Margaret.

Henry Tudor, meanwhile, had not been idle. Having gained French backing for a second invasion, he and a small force, many of them mercenaries, sailed from Harfleur on 1 August 1485, to take a second try at toppling Richard III from the throne. This time, they succeeded. Henry Tudor the obscure exile had become King Henry VII.

One of the king's first orders would be to have Sir Robert Willoughby conduct Warwick from the north to London, accompanied, most likely, by Margaret.[14] For Margaret, it was a new beginning, albeit an uncertain one. For her brother, it was the beginning of the end.

2

A NEW ORDER

What Margaret thought of the death of her uncle Richard III we cannot know, but as she rode south on the orders of the new King Henry, she must have done so with some trepidation. Orphaned, with her closest relative a boy younger than herself, she had no powerful male relations to speak up for her, nor could her female ones be of much help. Her paternal grandmother, Cecily Neville, Duchess of York, was the mother of a defeated king; her maternal grandmother, Anne Beauchamp, Countess of Warwick, had been stripped of her lands during Edward IV's reign and had since been living as a dependent in Richard's household. Two of her father's sisters survived: Elizabeth, Duchess of Suffolk, and Margaret, Duchess of Burgundy. The Duchess of Suffolk's eldest son, John de la Pole, Earl of Lincoln, was in the awkward position of having supported Richard III; Margaret in volatile Burgundy had her own problems. Thus, young Margaret's future rested largely in the hands of a man neither she nor most other people in England had ever met.

Initially, Henry VII seems to have sent young Warwick, and probably Margaret as well, to live with his mother, the Countess of Richmond, as the countess was reimbursed the following February for having Warwick in her charge. With Warwick and Margaret were a number of other young people, including Edward IV's daughters (the eldest of whom, Elizabeth, would soon become Henry's queen) and Edward Stafford, whose father's beheading at Richard III's command had left him as the 3rd Duke of Buckingham.[1] Some time the following year, however, Warwick and Margaret were separated when Warwick was taken to the Tower of London to reside. For the rest of his life he would remain there, in effect as a prisoner. Henry VII was taking no chances. What made him decide at this particular moment that more secure custody was required for the boy is unknown, but it proved a wise, if ruthless, precaution.

Margaret, however, lived a rather different life. Too young during Edward IV's reign to play an active role at court, and living far from court during most of Richard III's reign, she became a familiar face at the ceremonies of the first Tudor court.

Henry VII and Elizabeth of York, who had married on 18 January 1486, wasted no time in conceiving their first child, Arthur, who arrived – possibly prematurely – on 20 September 1486. At the baby's christening, held at Winchester on 24 September, 'my lady Margaret of Clarence' was prominent among the guests. As Margaret watched the anointment of the little prince, clothed in his mantel of crimson cloth of gold furred with ermine, she could not have guessed that it was not this infant but his brother, who arrived with considerably less fanfare five years later, who would have the greatest impact on her life.[2]

One of those playing a prominent role at the christening had been John de la Pole, Earl of Lincoln, who helped Cecily, Elizabeth of York's younger sister, carry Prince Arthur. Lincoln's mother, Elizabeth, Duchess of Suffolk, was a sister of Edward IV, Richard III and George, Duke of Clarence, making Lincoln and his numerous siblings Margaret's first cousins. Lincoln's parents (his father, the Duke of Suffolk, was also named John de la Pole) had managed to avoid getting caught up in the internecine struggles of the past several decades – an impressive feat – and had transitioned smoothly from Edward IV's reign to Richard III's to Henry VII's. Lincoln himself had stayed loyal to Richard III during his brief reign; it has even been speculated that Richard regarded him as his heir after the death of Richard's son, although any expectation would likely have been theoretical given the likelihood that Richard would have remarried after his queen's death in 1485.

Although Lincoln had apparently fought at Bosworth for Richard, having been mistakenly reported among the dead,[3] the victorious Henry had made no moves against him, neither attainting him nor imprisoning him. Instead, Henry had welcomed him to his court, and Lincoln had dutifully played his part at Henry's coronation.[4] In the spring of 1486, when Francis, Viscount Lovell, a supporter of Richard III, led an ill-supported rebellion in Yorkshire against Henry, Lincoln accompanied Henry to York to put it down. He was among the commissioners named to enquire into related conspiracies in Warwickshire and Worcestershire.[5]

But no sooner had Henry VII put down this rebellion than another conspiracy arose, with Margaret's brother – or, that is, a young man pretending to be him – at its focus.[6] The details remain murky, but in the winter of 1486/7, a boy known to history by the perhaps fictitious name of Lambert Simnel turned up in Yorkist-friendly Dublin under the tutelage of a priest named Simonds, who claimed that his charge was the Earl of Warwick. The supposed Warwick gained adherents, causing Henry VII's council, meeting in February 1487, to decide that the real Warwick, living his monotonous life in the Tower, should be shown to the great and the good. Accordingly, in the words of Polydore Vergil, Henry 'commanded that Edward, son to the Duke of Clarence, be brought out the Tower and led through the middle of the city to St. Paul's cathedral. This young man showing himself to everybody, as he had been instructed, and participated in a thanksgiving and the rest of the rites, and at same time had conversation with many lords and particularly with those thought to be participants in the conspiracy, so that they might more readily understand that the Irish were foolishly making an uprising because of a vain thing.'[7] As is usually the case – chroniclers of the time seldom concerned themselves with the affairs of women, much less young girls – we have no idea what Margaret made of this.

Warwick's brief excursion, however, did not have the desired effect. Shortly afterwards, the Earl of Lincoln, who had hitherto given Henry no obvious concern, took off to Burgundy, where Margaret, Duchess of Burgundy, was happy to host the king's enemies. There Lincoln joined Viscount Lovell, who had fled following his abortive rebellion of 1486. With a mercenary army in tow, Lincoln and Lovell made their way to Ireland, where they met up with the ten-year-old pretender, who perhaps now may have been wondering what he had got himself into, and crowned him as 'Edward VI' on 24 May 1487.

With their new king in tow, the rebels landed at Furness, Lancashire, in June 1487. Henry, however, was well prepared for the invasion, and on 16 June defeated the rebels near East Stoke. Lincoln was killed in the battle, and Lovell fled, probably into Scotland, his days of kingmaking over. The hapless Lambert Simnel was put to work in the royal kitchens and later became a royal falconer. He may have eventually fathered a son: Richard Simnel, canon of St Osith's in Essex.

While King Henry had been dealing with this strife, Queen Elizabeth had been carrying out her duties as queen uncrowned, to the dismay of some who thought the delay unseemly. With England at peace, Henry turned his thoughts to her coronation. But first, it appears, he had Margaret's future to settle.

As with so much of Margaret's early years, the date of her marriage is uncertain.[8] As Hazel Pierce notes, although a date as late as 1494 has been suggested, Margaret's first child, Henry, was born in June 1492, placing the date of her marriage no later than 1491. Pierce, however, has argued for around November 1487, for in the heralds' account of the queen's coronation Margaret is referred to by her married name. This would appear to settle the matter – but as Pierce also points out, things are not so straightforward, as the account of the coronation does not survive in its original version. It is possible, then, that the copyist gave Margaret the name she later bore rather than the name she bore in 1487. Nonetheless, in light of the events of 1486–87, it appears likely that Henry, wary of what use young Margaret might be put to, decided to marry her off to a loyal subject sooner rather than later.

The subject's name was Richard Pole, a half-cousin of the king. He was born in 1458 or 1459 to Geoffrey Pole, Esq. and Edith St John of Bletsoe. Edith was the daughter of Sir Oliver St John and Margaret Beauchamp. After Oliver St John's death, Margaret married John Beaufort, Duke of Somerset. Their only child, Margaret Beaufort, was the mother of Henry VII. Thus, Edith St John was Margaret Beaufort's older half-sister. Despite Margaret's considerably higher rank than her St John half-siblings, she was close to the family and even memorialised a descent of the St John family in a piece of needlework which she presented to her half-brother John St John upon his marriage.[9]

Richard Pole had soon reaped the rewards of his royal kinship. Soon after the Battle of Bosworth he was made a commissioner of the peace in Buckinghamshire, and on 22 October 1485, not long before Henry's coronation on 30 October 1485, he was appointed an esquire of the body for life. In 1486, he was made the constable of Harlech Castle and sheriff of Merioneth, again for life.

Hazel Pierce has suggested that Henry arranged Margaret's marriage to Richard Pole at the same time that he arranged that of Elizabeth of York's younger sister Cecily to John, Viscount Welles. Welles was yet another relation of the king through Margaret Beauchamp, who had married Lionel, Lord Welles, after the death of John Beaufort, Duke of Somerset. Like the St John family, John Welles was close to his half-sister Margaret Beaufort. Whereas Richard Pole had taken no part in the upheavals of Richard III's reign, John Welles had thrown his lot in with Henry Tudor early and had shared his exile after the rebellion of 1483 failed.

If the marriages did take place in 1487, as Pierce suggests, it was probably in November. Parliament met that month, and Queen Elizabeth was due to be crowned on 25 November, ensuring that plenty of the nobility would be on hand to attend the weddings. We know nothing about the ceremony itself, save that the king and queen were present.[10]

As Margaret had turned fourteen only a few months before, the marriage (assuming it did take place in 1487) probably was not consummated immediately. Although noblewomen often were married at what strikes us as shockingly young ages, society did appreciate the dangers of early childbirth, meaning that a girl might wait until she was in her mid to late teens to consummate her marriage. The king's mother, Margaret Beaufort, Countess of Richmond, was well aware of such risks: married at twelve, she had borne her first, and only, child at age thirteen, and it has often been speculated that physical trauma from the experience prevented her from bearing more children. Later, when her oldest granddaughter was proposed as a bride for Scotland's James IV, the countess would fret that sending the girl to Scotland might tempt James to consummate the match too early.[11] Quite possibly the Countess of Richmond felt a similar solicitude for Richard Pole's bride, for it would not be until 1492 that Margaret bore her first child.

Any weddings during this period would have been outshone by Elizabeth's coronation, a spectacular event in which both Richard Pole and Margaret took part.[12] On the eve of the coronation, Elizabeth, clad in white cloth of gold with her 'fair yellow hair' hanging loose, rode in a litter (as elegantly trapped as she) from the Tower of London to Westminster, in accordance with custom. Twelve knights of the body, Richard Pole among them, took turns bearing, in shifts of four, a canopy over the queen's litter. Behind the queen rode numerous ladies; Margaret, though not singled out for mention, was likely one of them.

By custom, Henry did not take a visible part at his queen's coronation at Westminster Abbey the next day. He watched the proceedings, however, from a 'goodly stage', which was erected on the right side of the church between the pulpit and the high altar and which was concealed from public view. With the king were 'my lady his mother and a goodly sight of ladies and gentlewomen attending upon her, as my lady Margaret Pole, daughter to the Duke of Clarence, and many other'. A great feast in two courses followed, with every imaginable meat, fish and fowl on the menu (goat, peacock and seal were among the offerings). The meal ended with a serving of jelly shaped into castles, followed by a 'subtlety', a spectacular dish of sugar, pastry and inedible material made to dazzle the eye. Margaret may have dined with the king and his mother, who again were eating in a specially constructed stage, or she may have been among the 'noble gentlewomen' dining in the hall.

The next day, following Mass in St Stephen's chapel, the queen kept her estate in the Parliament chamber, Margaret Beaufort at her right, and the Duchess of Bedford and the Lady Cecily on her left. Seated at the side table were the Duchess of Suffolk, the Duchess of Norfolk, the Countess of Oxford, the Countess of Wiltshire, the Countess of Rivers, the Countess of Nottingham, 'my lady Margaret Pole', Lady Strange, Lady Grey, Lady La Warre, Lady Dudley, Lady Mountjoy and 'many other ladies', including Lady Katherine Grey, Lady Katherine Vaux, Lady Elizabeth Guildford, Lady Elizabeth Wingfield and Lady Elizabeth Longville. Following dinner, the queen and the ladies danced. The ceremonies ended the next day when the queen removed to Greenwich so that Parliament could resume its business.

Following this excitement, Margaret may have continued to reside at court while she matured sufficiently to consummate her marriage. She continued to be prominent at the grand events there: at the feast of St George in 1488, she was among the ladies waiting upon the queen and the king's mother. That December, she was one of a host of ladies keeping Christmas at Sheen Palace with the royal family.[13]

Because Margaret had no land of her own, she would have started her married life with Richard Pole on his own estates, which at the onset of Henry VII's reign were modest: the manors of Medmenham, Hallonds, Withmere, Ellesborough and Stoke Mandeville in Buckinghamshire, which brought in about 50 pounds per year. After the Battle of Stoke Field, Richard Pole was likely granted the manors of Fifield and Long Wittenham in Oxfordshire, confiscated from the dead Earl of Lincoln. His chief residence was Bockmer, located in the manor of Medmenham. Later, Henry granted him Stourton Castle in Wales.[14]

Once Margaret began to live with her husband, she settled into the traditional wifely role of providing him with children. Margaret had at least five, with the eldest, Henry, arriving in 1492, followed by Arthur, Ursula, Reginald and Geoffrey. Ludovico Beccadelli, the secretary of the most famous of these children, Reginald, maintained that there were six children, two of them girls; if this was true, the second girl died too young to leave a mark in the historical record.[15]

Meanwhile, Richard Pole continued to prosper under Henry VII. In 1486, he was made constable of Harlech Castle; in 1488, constable of Conwy Castle; in 1495, constable of Caernarfon and Beaumaris castles. He was also appointed to various commissions, and in 1490 was made chamberlain of North Wales for life. In 1495, Henry made him justice of North Wales; Henry's trusted uncle, Jasper Tudor, Duke of Bedford, held the same position in South Wales. A particularly striking indication of the king's regard for Richard was his appointment as chamberlain of the king's heir, Arthur, by March 1493. Richard received the Order of the Garter in April 1499, the highest chivalric honour in England and one that has been described by S. B. Chrimes as 'the ultimate mark of honour favoured by Henry VII'.[16]

While Richard Pole basked in royal favour and Margaret bore his children, the Earl of Warwick's doom was fast approaching. Since the failure of the Lambert Simnel uprising, Warwick had been immured in the Tower. This was not necessarily meant to have been a permanent state of affairs, for in 1488 he had been allowed to witness a document in Warwickshire – perhaps a sign that Henry VII was considering his release.[17] The next pretender, however, would soon put an end to even these feeble hopes for Warwick.

Who precisely 'Perkin Warbeck' was remains controversial, but he was most likely born in Tournai, France, to Jehan de Werbecque and Nicaise Farou.[18] Working as a silk merchant, in 1491 Warbeck eventually landed in Cork in Ireland, where he caught the eye of diehard Yorkists who saw in him a likely pretender. This time, the role to be played was that of Richard, Duke of York, who with his older brother Edward V had disappeared during Richard III's reign. Warbeck was briefly supported by the French, but then moved on to the more promising ground of Burgundy, where Edward IV and Richard III's sister, Margaret, was the dowager duchess. Maximillian, King of the Romans, who was married to Margaret's stepdaughter, backed a failed invasion of England in 1495, but James IV, the King of Scotland, lent his own backing to the pretender, even going so far to marry him in 1496 to his relative Lady Katherine Gordon, the daughter of George, Earl of Huntley. After another failed attack in 1497, Warbeck went into sanctuary at Beaulieu Abbey, but surrendered in exchange for his life.

Having confessed his imposture and undergone the humiliation of being paraded around London, the captive Warbeck joined Henry VII's court, where he was kept under close surveillance and separated from his wife (who stayed with the queen), but otherwise treated rather well for a man who had tried to unseat a ruling king. In June 1498, however, Warbeck escaped from Westminster Palace. Within a few days, he was recaptured and sent to the Tower.

Meanwhile, another plot was brewing: this one involving Robert Cleymond, a servant of the imprisoned Earl of Warwick who in February 1498 had met with a John Fynche, a London haberdasher who told Cleymond of a prophesy involving the restoration of the earl, and a Thomas Astwode, who had been condemned to death for treason in 1495 but had been pardoned. In July 1498, soon after Perkin Warbeck was imprisoned in the Tower, John Williams, a servant of the Earl of Warwick, introduced Astwode to the young earl. Astwode promised the earl 'to do you good and help to put you in your right'.[19] Soon – according to the government – the imposter Perkin Warbeck was plotting with Cleymond, Astwode and Warwick to topple King Henry from this throne.

Whether the conspiracy was spontaneous or, as some have suggested, manufactured in part or entirely by the government to entrap Warbeck and Warwick, the young earl was ill-equipped for such intrigues. Several decades later, the chronicler Edward Hall would write that Warwick, '[b]eing kept in the Tower from his tender age, that is to say from his first year of the king to this fifteenth year, out of all company of men and sight of beasts, in so much that he could not discern a goose from a capon'.[20] Quoted out of context, this statement has been taken by some to indicate that Warwick was mentally deficient from birth; yet Hall's meaning simply seems to be that Edward, having been imprisoned since the beginning of Henry's reign, was naive and unworldly. Having been a prisoner since childhood, he had never had the chance to exercise judgment.

Sir Simon Digby, the lieutenant of the Tower, learned of the plot in early August. The king and his council, informed of the plot, did nothing, allowing the case against the principals to build. On 12 November 1499, the king consulted his councillors, who agreed that Warwick and Warbeck had to die.

A common belief is that Warwick's fate was sealed by the need to assure Ferdinand and Isabella, whose daughter, Katherine of Aragon, was pledged to marry Prince Arthur, that England was free of the threat of future civil war. As Edmund Hall, writing several decades later, stated, 'The fame after his death sprang abroad, [that] Ferdinand king of Spain would never make full conclusion of the matrimony to be had between Prince Arthur and the lady Katherine his daughter nor send her into England as long as this earl lived. For he imagined that as long as any earl of Warwick lived, that England should never be cleansed or purged of civil war and privy sedition, so much was the name of Warwick in other regions had in fear and jealousy.'[21] This may well have been the case, although the appearance in early 1499 of a second Warwick imposter, one Ralph Wilford, and astrological predictions of coming trouble played their role as well. In March 1499, Don Pedro De Ayala wrote to Ferdinand and Isabella of the prognostications that 'Henry has aged so much during the last two weeks that he seems to be twenty years older'.[22]

Following a trial on 16 November 1499, Perkin Warbeck was hanged at Tyburn on 23 November. Warwick, in turn, was brought to trial before John de Vere, Earl of Oxford, and other lords at Westminster, as befit a peer of the realm, on 21 November. He confessed to the charges against him and was sentenced to the traitor's death of hanging, drawing and quartering. Such a sentence was usually reduced to a beheading (the preferred means of execution for a man of noble blood), and this held true in Warwick's case. On 28 November, twenty-four-year-old Warwick was beheaded outside the Tower of London. The king paid for the interment of his head and body at Bisham Abbey, the resting place of his ancestors. Two months later, the Spanish ambassador, Rodrigo de Puebla, crowed that 'not a doubtful drop of royal blood remains in this kingdom, except the true blood of the king and queen, and above all, that of the lord prince Arthur'.[23]

Margaret, of course, remained in the kingdom, but as a female who had been married to a loyal subject, her own royal blood was of little concern. We can assume that she grieved for her brother, but no one recorded her reaction to his execution. How well she knew him is another question. She and her brother had lived apart for years, and we do not know whether they communicated after he was imprisoned. Later, Margaret would declare that her brother had neither 'experience nor knowledge of the worldly policies nor of the laws of this realm',[24] which could indicate that Margaret had been in contact with her brother during his last years; alternatively, Margaret could simply be repeating what she had heard from others.

Whatever the depth of Margaret's sorrow, there would soon be a welcome distraction: her son Reginald was born in March 1500 in Stourton Castle. The following year there would be a distraction on a national level: a royal wedding.

3

TWO WIDOWS

Before Katherine of Aragon came to England, she had already been married to Arthur for two years by proxy. Richard Pole, in his role of Arthur's chamberlain, had played a role in the ceremony, which took place in May 1499 and was presided over by John Arundel, Bishop of Coventry and Litchfield: 'The Prince of Wales took, with his right hand, the right hand of Doctor De Puebla; and Richard [Pole], Lord Chamberlain of the Prince, and Knight of the Garter, held the hands of both in his hands. In this position, the Prince declared that he accepted De Puebla in the name and as the proxy of the Princess Katharine, and the Princess Katharine as his lawful and undoubted wife.'[1] Later, Richard Pole commemorated the event by commissioning a rood screen for Aberconwy Abbey, later the Church of St Mary and All Saints, in Caernarvonshire, close to Conwy Castle.[2]

Born on 16 December 1485, Katherine was just a few months younger than the dynasty she would marry into. We tend to think of her as she was in later life, the formidable matron battling to preserve her marriage or the defeated, lonely figure dying in poverty at Kimbolton Castle, but when she arrived in England in October 1501, she was a pretty, auburn-haired girl of fifteen, well equipped to charm her future subjects.

Katherine married Arthur, who had recently turned fifteen, on 14 November 1501, amid pomp and pageantry on a grand scale. Margaret is not mentioned by name as a participant in these festivities, but then neither are most of the titled ladies one would expect to be present, so this means little. Given her breeding and her husband's importance in the prince's household, it is highly unlikely she would have been absent. Quite likely she was with the 'goodly company ... of countesses, baronesses, and many other honourable gentlewomen' who went to meet Katherine after she landed, and was among those 'ladies, and other gentlewomen to a great and goodly number' present at the wedding. Perhaps she was among the 'divers ladies of England' with Katherine when Henry VII showed the homesick princess his library of 'many goodly pleasant books' before allowing her and their ladies to choose some fine jewels for themselves.[3] If in all of this Margaret gained any knowledge of the answer to the question that was to assume burning importance three decades later – whether the two adolescents had consummated their marriage – she kept it to herself.

Arthur's official residence was at Ludlow, to which he returned with his new bride on 21 December 1501, accompanied, of course, by Richard Pole. Probably Margaret went there as well; at the very least, she may have visited her husband at Ludlow from time to time and furthered her acquaintance with Katherine. If the women believed that Margaret's brother had been killed so as to conclude Katherine's marriage to Arthur then this might have put them on an awkward footing, but as neither had grown up around rulers noted for overdelicacy in dealing with their opponents it is unlikely that Margaret harboured any resentment of the young princess. Certainly their friendship would prosper in the years to come.

But the couple's stay at Ludlow ended in tragedy when, on 2 April 1502, young Arthur died of the 'most pitiful disease and sickness'. Richard Pole, as the boy's chamberlain, had the grim duty of writing to King Henry to announce the news, which was broken to the king in person by the king's confessor.[4] At the funeral ceremonies, which culminated in Arthur's burial at Worcester Cathedral, Richard Pole was one of the eight official mourners.[5] A widow at sixteen, Katherine of Aragon returned to London, where she remained in limbo for over seven years while Henry VII and her parents wrangled over her dowry and the possibility of her marriage to the English king's only surviving son, Henry.

With Arthur's death, Richard Pole went back to his other duties in Wales, and Margaret back to the duties of raising her growing family. Sadly, Margaret soon had another loss to endure: shortly before 20 October 1504, Richard Pole, aged about forty-five or forty-six, died. The marriage appears, from what we can tell from the records, to have been a happy one: Margaret's possessions in 1538 included her husband's celure and tester embroidered with garters, a cushion bearing his arms, and silver and gilt bowls in which his device was placed side by side with those of the Duke of Clarence. In 1536, writing to her son Reginald to complain of his actions toward Henry VIII, she told him, 'There went never the death of thy father or of any child so nigh my heart.'[6]

Grief, however, was not the only problem Margaret faced after her husband's death. She may have been pregnant with her son Geoffrey at the time, and she was certainly short on funds, as Richard's salary from his various lucrative offices had ended with his death, and her jointure from her husband's estates would not have been substantial, given that the total value of his estates was probably only about £170 per year. With Charles Somerset, an illegitimate cousin of Henry VII who was probably acting as an executor of Richard Pole, on 20 October 1504, Margaret had to borrow £40 from the king for her husband's burial. The money was to be repaid from the profits of Richard Pole's lands, most of which, save for Margaret's jointure properties, were in the hands of the king during the minority of Henry Pole, now a royal ward. Two months later, the king granted Margaret £52 6s 8d for her 'finding [i.e., support] and raiment'.[7]

Margaret's solution to her problem was similar to that of many highborn widows: to take lodgings at a house of religion.[8] The House of the Minoresses without Aldgate in London had housed many such widows, most notably Elizabeth, Duchess of Norfolk, whose daughter, Anne Mowbray, had been the child bride of Edward IV's second son, Richard, Duke of York. Edward IV's own queen, Elizabeth Woodville, had retreated to Bermondsey Abbey in 1487. Margaret's choice, as noted by her contemporary Richard Morisyne and later confirmed by documentary evidence found by historian Sue Powell, was the Bridgettine monastery of Syon Abbey, which housed both men and women religious. Located on the River Thames west of London, the abbey was among the wealthiest in England, with a fine library. Henry VIII would later lodge his troublesome niece, Margaret Douglas, there after she made a secret marriage to Lord Thomas Howard, and his fifth wife, Katherine Howard, stayed there for a time after being accused of adultery.

Margaret Beaufort, the king's mother, helped support Margaret at Syon, and often visited the abbey, where she had a goddaughter, Margaret Windsor (a future prioress there), as well. As noted by Powell, Margaret Beaufort's accounts show payments to Margaret Pole from May 1505 to May 1509, a month before Margaret Beaufort's death. At least two of her children were at the abbey: her daughter, Ursula, who is mentioned by name in the accounts, and presumably her baby, Geoffrey. The records refer to 'two women nurses to my lady Pole's two children'; if, as Powell suggests, these two nurses were wet nurses, one of the children may have been the second daughter mentioned by Ludovico Beccadelli, as noted in Chapter 2. Henry and Arthur, the oldest two Pole boys, might have been living at court or in a noble household, although there is no record of this. Reginald from age seven attended the Carthusians' grammar school at Sheen, so from 1507 on he would have been absent from his mother's household.[9]

Meanwhile, on 11 February 1503 – her thirty-seventh birthday – Elizabeth of York had died, leaving behind a grieving king whose personality hardened with the loss of a woman he seems to have truly loved. Margaret Pole's grandmothers, Anne Beauchamp, Countess of Warwick, and Cecily, Duchess of York, had died in 1492 and 1495 respectively; the latter's will, perhaps out of prudence given the rebellions of the 1480s and 1490s, made no mention of either Margaret or her brother, although it is possible that Cecily gave gifts to Margaret during her lifetime.[10] None of these deaths seem to have made much difference in Margaret's life, at least that we can discern from the distance of five centuries. But the next death, that of Henry VII on 21 April 1509, would change everything for Margaret.

4

COUNTESS OF SALISBURY

Ironically, some of the people who would suffer most under Henry VIII were the most delighted to see the eighteen-year-old ascend to the throne. Thomas More, one of the most distinguished casualties of Henry's reign, rhapsodized, 'This day is the limit of our slavery, the beginning of our freedom, the end of sadness, the source of joy, for this day consecrates a young man who is the everlasting glory of our time and makes him your king – the only king who is worthy to rule not merely a single people but the whole world – such a king as will wipe the tears from every eye and put joy in the place of our long distress.'[1] Nobles such as Edward Stafford, Duke of Buckingham, who had been put under heavy financial obligations to the Crown ('a reign of fiscal terror', as historian David Starkey has it),[2] were relieved of their burdens; Buckingham would be relieved of his head a few years later. Only Henry VII's hated councillors Richard Empson and Edmund Dudley, who were promptly arrested and later executed, had any cause to complain of the new king.

No one, however, benefited from the change of regime more than Henry VIII's forlorn sister-in-law, Katherine of Aragon. Her years of uncertainty and relative poverty ended on 11 June 1509 when Henry married her at Greenwich. The ceremony was small and private, as would be Henry's other five weddings; the show was to come on 24 June, when Henry was crowned as king and Katherine as his consort.

Margaret too found her fortunes transformed by the young new king. In the wake of her tragic death, it is easy to forget, and is often forgotten, that at the outset of his reign Henry was well-disposed to her – as, indeed, he was to his other maternal relatives. As David Starkey points out, generosity toward his Yorkist relatives helped underscore the new king's break with his father's regime, and there may have been personal considerations as well in that the king, who was said to strongly resemble his grandfather Edward IV, simply liked his mother's side of the family.[3]

So that Margaret could attend the coronation, she was lodged in London with a Lady Williams, who received £26 13s 4d for Margaret's board. For attending upon Katherine at the coronation, Margaret received the twelve yards of cloth allotted to a countess – an omen of things to come. Along with such ladies as the Duke of Buckingham's sisters, Elizabeth and Anne Stafford, and the countesses of Surrey, Shrewsbury, Essex and Derby, Margaret became one of the queen's ladies-in-waiting. Her eldest son, Henry, also waited upon the queen at the coronation in some capacity.[4] Edmund Hall described the coronation, and the procession from the Tower to Westminster the day before it, in loving and breathless detail:

The features of his body, his goodly personage, his amiable visage, princely countenance, with the noble qualities of his royal estate, to every man known needs no rehearsal, considering, that for lack of cunning, I cannot express the gifts of grace and of nature, that God hath endowed, him with all: yet partly, to describe his apparel, it is to be noted, his grace wore in his upperest apparel, a robe of Crimson Velvet, furred with ermines, his Jacket or coat of raised gold, the Placard embroidered with Diamonds Rubies, Emeralds, great Pearls, and other rich Stones, a great Bauderike about his neck, of great Balasses. The Trapper of his Horse, Damask gold, with a deep purfell of Anuyns, his knights and Esquires for his body in Crimson Velvet, and all the gentlemen, with other of his chapel, and all his officers, and household servants, were appareled in Scarlet. The Barons of the five Ports, bore the Canopy, or cloth of estate: For to recite unto you, the great estates by name, the order of their going, the number of the lords Spiritual and temporal, Knights, Esquires, and Gentlemen, and of their costly and rich apparel, of several devises, and fashions, who took up his horse best, or who was richest beseen, it would ask long time, and yet I should omit many things, and fail of the number, for they were very many: wherefore I pass over, but this I dare well say, there was no lack or scarcity of cloth of Tissue, cloth of Gold, cloth of Silver, Broderie, or of Goldsmiths' works: but in more plenty and abundance, then hath been seen, or read of at any time before ...

Then next following in order, came the Queen's retinue, as Lords, Knights, Esquires and gentlemen in their degrees, well mounted, and richly appareled in Tissues, cloth of Gold, of Silver, Tinsels, and Velvet Embroidered, fresh and goodly to behold. The Queen then by name Katherine, sitting in her Litter, borne by two White Palfreys the Litter covered, and richly appareled, and the Palfreys Trapped in White cloth of gold, her person appareled in white Satin Embroidered, her hair hanging down to her back, of a very great length, beautiful and goodly to behold, and on her head a Coronal, set with many rich orient stones. Next after, six honorable personages on White Palfreys, all appareled in Cloth of Gold, and then a Chariot covered, and the Ladies therein, all appareled in Cloth of Gold. And another sort of Ladies, and then another Chariot, then the Ladies next the Chariot, and so in order, every after their degrees in cloth of Gold, Cloth of Silver, Tinsels, and Velvet, with Embroideries, every couplement of the said Chariots, and the draught harnesses, were powdered with ermines, mixed with cloth of Gold: and with much joy and honour came to Westminster where high preparation made, as well for the said coronation, also for the solemn feasts and jousts thereupon to be had and done.

The morrow following being Sunday, and also Midsummer day, this noble prince with his Queen, at time convenient under their Canopies borne by the Barons of the five Port went from the said Palace, to Westminster Abbey upon clothe, called vulgarly cloth of Ray, the which cloth was cut and spoiled, by the rude and common people, immediately after their repair into the Abbey, where, according to the sacred observance, and ancient custom, his grace with the Queen, were anointed and crowned, by the archbishop of Canterbury, with other prelates of the realm there present, and the nobility, with a great multitude of Commons of the same. It was demanded of the people, whether they would receive, obey, and take the same most noble Prince, for their king, who with great reverence, love, and desire, said and cried, 'Yea, Yea'![5]

In the midst of all of this splendour, Margaret could have hardly guessed that two decades later, a second queen would be crowned in equal grandeur as Henry's consort.

Having made a place for Margaret at his and his queen's coronation, Henry's next action was, on 31 July 1509, to grant her an annuity of £100.[6] As will be seen in the next chapter, Henry also treated her children generously. But Margaret's fortunes were truly transformed three years later when the king, at Margaret's petition, restored her to the earldom of Salisbury and created her Countess of Salisbury in her own right.

Such an action went well beyond giving Margaret a place at court and an annuity. Reginald Pole's explanation for Henry's actions, set forth in a letter to Edward Seymour, Duke of Somerset, then serving as the Protector for Henry VIII's son, Edward VI, was as follows:

[I]n his first Parliament, [Henry VIII] restored to my lady mother the greater part of her revenues on this condition, that she was to pardon the King, his father, for the death of her brother, a man perfectly innocent, who was the last Earl of Warwick. This the King did, because his father, Henry VIL, being at the extremity, and by the grace of God repenting of the acts of injustice committed by him during his reign, and amongst the rest calling to mind one of the most notable done to our uncle the Earl of Warwick, and to our family and wishing for pardon from God, and from those he had offended, ordered the restitution to my lady mother of her revenues intrusted to the King his son, who then, as a Prince obedient to God and to his father, restored her revenues to my mother, with the condition mentioned by me, namely, that she was to forgive the King his father the injuries received from him. And this was told her in the Council, when summoned for the purpose of hearing the will of the King, which was, that her own property should be restored to her; and when asked if with her whole heart she forgave King Henry VII. the death of her brother, and all the injuries which he had done her, she replied that not only was she content to forgive all the past, but acknowledged herself very much bound to pray God for his Majesty.

Reginald Pole went on to tell the Protector:

I will tell you of the grievous trouble and remorse which [Katherine of Aragon] had to endure, as frequently alluded to by herself, always thinking of this, namely, that a great part of her troubles emanated from God, not through any fault of her own, but for the salvation of her soul; and that the Divine justice thus punished the sin of her father King Ferdinand, for when he commenced negotiating her marriage with Prince Arthur, the eldest son of the King of England, some disturbances took place at the time, owing to the favour and goodwill borne by the people to my mother's brother the Earl of Warwick, of whom we have made mention above, who being the son of the Duke of Clarence, brother of King Edward, became, by the death of that King's sons, next heir to the English crown. King Ferdinand, having by the agreements to conclude his daughter's marriage at that time, made a difficulty about it, saying he would not give her to one who was not secure in his own kingdom; and thus, by inciting the

King to do what he already desired spontaneously, he was the cause of the death of that innocent Earl, who had no more blame in those commotions, nor could anything else be laid to his charge, save the danger which the King in Council alleged had already befallen him in part, through the existence of the said Earl; and in addition to this having heard the opinion of the King of Spain, he did that deed, of which (as I have already said) he so greatly repented on his death-bed.

But the Divine justice did not permit so iniquitous an act of injustice to remain unpunished, for at the end of six months Prince Arthur died, nor could he any longer enjoy the wife who had been given him by such bad counsel, and she was then re-married to the King's other son, who succeeded to his crown. To these causes that good Princess said that she attributed in great part the annoyances and distresses endured by her, confessing that she was therefore very much bound to recompense and requite us for the detriment we had received on her account (although she was not in the least to blame for it), and to show us every kindness, having found by experience that in all her sorrows and afflictions, from no family of the realm had she ever received greater consolation than from ours, although for her sake we had received so many injuries.[7]

Reginald Pole's letter cannot be taken entirely at face value, however. Then in exile, Reginald had made overtures toward the Protector and had met with a less than enthusiastic response, injuring his pride and impelling him to suggest that 'Edward should beg pardon of him on account of Henry's injuries to Pole and his family, not he of Edward'.[8] It behoved him, therefore, through Somerset, to heap guilt upon Edward VI for the actions of his forbears. In fact, Henry's restoration of Margaret was a gesture typical of the king in the golden early days of his reign. In 1510, Henry had made his cousin Henry Stafford, the Duke of Buckingham's younger brother, the Earl of Wiltshire. He had restored another cousin, William Courtenay, to the earldom of Devon in 1511. Thus, it seems that Henry was simply acting in accordance with his already noted policy of building good relations with the nobility in general, and his Yorkist relations in particular.[9] Furthermore, Katherine of Aragon, quite apart from any nagging sense of guilt she might have felt about Warwick's execution years before, thought highly of Margaret, in whose care she would later entrust her only child, and likely spoke favourably of her to the king.

Margaret's petition for restoration is her only known comment upon the fate of her brother Warwick. Alas, the petition, clearly drafted by someone with expertise in such matters, is dispassionate and straightforward. Prudently, Margaret does not absolve her brother from blame, but simply argues that he did not know what he was doing: 'Which Edward most gracious sovereign lord, was always from his childhood being of the age of eight years until the time of his decease remaining and kept in ward and restrained from his liberty as well in the Tower of London as in other places having no experience nor knowledge of the worldly policies nor of the laws of this realm, so that if any offence were by him done concerning such matters specified in the said act of attainder it was rather by innocence than of any malicious purpose.'[10]

Although Parliament granted Margaret's petition on 4 February 1512, Margaret had to pay a fee (as was customary) in order to enter her lands, in this case 5,000 marks for lands that Hazel Pierce has estimated as being worth over £2,000.[11] Margaret paid the first instalment of £1,000, probably through borrowed funds, in May 1513 and entered her manors the following January. The bulk of her estates were in Hampshire, Somerset, Devon and Buckinghamshire, although they spanned seventeen counties in England and included holdings in Wales, the Isle of Wight and Calais. Pierce estimates that her income made her the fifth- or sixth-wealthiest English noble of her day.

Naturally, Margaret did not confine herself to one residence or spend time at all of her estates; rather, she spent most of her time at Clavering in Essex, Bisham at Berkshire, Le Herber in London and Warblington in Hampshire. Only earthworks remain of the moated castle at Clavering, which stood near St Mary & St Clement's Church.[12] Bisham, where Margaret's grandfather Richard Neville, Earl of Warwick, and her brother were buried, was desirable enough for Henry VIII himself to reserve it for his own use after Margaret's attainder. It was purchased in 1552 by Sir Thomas Hoby, whose surveyor noted that the mansion house occupied by Margaret, which sat on the River Thames and adjoined what was before the Dissolution a monastery, was built partly of stone and partly of timber, with a tiled roof. There was a 'hall with a chimney, and at the lower end of the same is a pantry, a butlerly, a kitchen, a larder, and a little wood yard. At the over end of the same ascending by a fair half pace is a great chamber with an inner chamber and six other chambers and lodging upon a quadrant, and underneath these chambers at the foot of the said half pace is a wine cellar and a quarant cloister with certain small lodgings on every side of the same, the which cloister leadeths unto two little garden plots.' Edgar Powell reported that at the time of his writing, in 1902, Margaret's arms, impaled with her husband's, could be seen in the council chamber window.[13]

Margaret's London residence, Le Herber (also referred to in the records as the Erber), was a merchant's house that had passed in the fourteenth century into the hands of Margaret's forebears; Margaret may well have spent time there as a child, assuming that the little girl was brought to London by her parents on occasions. Situated in Dowgate south of the Church of St Mary Bothawe, and now covered in part by Cannon Street station, the house fronted on Dowgate, Chequer Lane and Bush Lane; some of its external buildings were leased to others for shops and residences. Accounts for repairs suggest that Margaret's chamber was on the east side of the house and overlooked the house's great garden (as opposed to its little garden). Margaret's son Henry had a chamber near the hay house. In 1520, Margaret paid a William Kellam 13s 4d for painting a new tabernacle which enclosed an image of the Virgin Mary; in a nice gesture, Margaret gave the man who made the old tabernacle his creation and 3s 4d. Margaret also made payments to the Abbot of Bermondsey and bought wax tapers for her neighbouring church, St Mary Bothawe, as well as for the church of St Mary Staining. Sums for mundane tasks such as paving, making repairs to Margaret's chamber, providing locks and bolts, and hauling dung are duly recorded as well.[14]

Nothing remains of Warblington Castle but a seven-storey gatehouse turret built in brick and stone. It is particularly irksome that the castle, dismantled during the Civil War, lies in ruins, for unlike Margaret's other primary residences it was built to her specifications – indeed, it was the 'only castle of the English Middle Ages unambiguously created in its entirety by a female patron'.[15] The written record, however, offers us a glimpse of the castle as it appeared in its glory days. In 1632, its current owner had it surveyed by William Luffe, who reported:

The site of the principal Manor House of Warblington is a very fair place, well moated about, built all with bricks and stones, and is of great receipt, built square, in length 200 feet and in breadth 200 feet, with a fair green court within, and buildings round the said court, with a fair gallery and divers chambers of great count, and four towers covered with lead, with a very great and spacious hall, parlour, and great chamber, and all other houses of office whatsoever, necessary for such a house, with a very fair chapel within the said house, and the place covered all with tiles and stones; and there is a fair green court before the gate of the said house, containing two acres of land, and there is a very spacious garden with pleasant walks adjoining, containing two acres of land, and near to the said place, groves of trees containing two acres of land, two orchards and two little meadow plots containing eight acres, and a fair fishpond near the said place, with a gate for wood and two barns, one of five bays the other of four bays, with stables and other outhouses.[16]

Margaret filled her castle (described as a 'new building' in accounts of 1517–18) with fine goods and furnishings.[17] An inventory of 1538 shows such items as seven hanging tapestries showing Ulysses' journey and nine depicting the discovery of Newfoundland. Margaret's coat of arms appeared on cushions, on a red sumpter cloth and on a piece over the chimney; the king's arms were also represented in five banqueting dishes of glass. For the musically inclined, there were several pairs of virginals. Carpets from Turkey and Flanders, hung on the windows, kept out the cold. The counterpane that was on Margaret's own bed was not deemed worthy of description by those taking the inventory, but a counterpane in a bedchamber within Margaret's own chamber had 'great borders with flowers and beasts'. Margaret or her staff could keep her accounts at a little desk for 'writings and reckonings for household and other things'. Perhaps the little coffer 'with silk for to set the young at work' had been used by Margaret's daughter or granddaughters. Court rolls and evidence were found in a coffer covered in seal skin. Books, their titles unrecorded, were found along with pillows, linen and glass. There was no shortage of plate, including a gilt cup decorated with a portcullis and roses, a salt cellar of gold garnished with stones and pearls, a salt of gold with a cardinal hat in the top, a spoon with an angel at the top, a silver-and-gilt standing cup with a man at the top, a silver-and-gilt standing cup with St John the Baptist at the top and a silver-and-gilt cup with nothing at the top.

It took considerable staff to run Margaret's large household. In 1538, she had a steward, a comptroller, three chaplains, six gentlemen waiters, two clerks of the kitchen, six yeomen of the chamber, two men who served as marshal of the hall and as usher of the hall, two men in the pantry, two men in the butlery, two men in the ewery, two men in the wardrobe plus a third at Bisham, two porters, two grooms of the chamber, three cooks, two bakers, a slaughterman, a cater, a tyler, a brewer, three boys of the kitchen, a housekeeper, a man who worked in the scullery, an almoner, a laundress, ten gentlemen servants and a man who was 'found of alms'. Bringing up the end of the list was an unnamed fool. Whether he was an 'innocent', that is, a person who was intellectually disabled or mentally ill, or an artificial fool, that is, an entertainer, is unknown, but clearly his presence indicates that the household of the aging countess was not a gloomy one.[18]

It was common for parents to place their preadolescent or adolescent daughters in a higher-ranking household so that the young ladies could polish their social graces and make useful connections. The most coveted placement, of course, was with the queen (and Henry VIII's multiple marriages at least had the merits of giving girls more openings for such placements than there otherwise would have been), but Margaret's household would have been highly desirable as well.[19] Many such placements involved near relations, and Margaret was no exception: of the eleven ladies who served her in 1538, five were her granddaughters: Margaret Stafford, the daughter of Ursula Pole; Winifred, the daughter of Henry Pole, Lord Montagu; Mary and Margaret Pole, Sir Arthur Pole's daughters; and Katherine Pole, Sir Geoffrey Pole's daughter. Three others also had close ties to Margaret: Johan Frankelyn was the wife of Oliver Frankelyn, Margaret's comptroller; Johan Chomeley was married to William Chomeley, who had formerly served Edward Stafford, Duke of Buckingham, and was being paid an annuity by Margaret; and Anne Ragland was married to Jerome Ragland, who served Lord Montagu. The other three, Elizabeth Cheyney, Dorothy Erneley and Alice Denstill, were likely members of local gentry families.[20]

As Hazel Pierce has noted, Margaret's servants stayed in her employ for long periods, indicating that Margaret had the knack of maintaining good relationships with them and a talent for choosing people who were qualified for their tasks. 'People' is used deliberately here, because four of Margaret's manorial officials were women. Margaret Frye served as reeve of Wilton after the death of Frye's husband, the previous reeve; Agnes Jacob was the reeve of Swainston on the Isle of Wight. Lady Elizabeth Hanshert acted as one of Margaret's bailiffs in Lincoln. Jane Lister, married to Richard Lister, Margaret's chief steward, was a receiver in Hampshire, Hertfordshire and Lincoln. Agnes Jacob and Lady Elizabeth Hanshert did employ male deputies, but the employment of four women in what was almost always a man's job is nonetheless striking.[21]

Not all of Margaret's concerns revolved around her earthy existence, of course: she also gave consideration to her final resting place, for which she chose Christchurch Priory in Hampshire. There she constructed a magnificent chantry, with receptacles for both her own coffin and a second one, presumably with the intent of moving her husband's body to lie beside hers. Built of Caen stone, and thought by some to be the design of Pietro Torrigiano, the chantry once bore Margaret's arms, which, as a royal commissioner matter-of-factly reported, were defaced after her imprisonment: 'In this church we found a chapel and a monument curiously made of Caen stone prepared by the late [*sic*] mother of Reginald Pole for her burial, which we have caused to be defaced and all the arms and badges to be deleted.' Margaret was not permitted to lie in the chantry that she had commissioned. In that she is similar to poet Percy Bysshe Shelley, who likewise has a monument at Christchurch without having been buried there.[22]

Margaret's restoration transformed her from a widow living in reduced circumstances to a wealthy woman. Nothing indicates that she ever considered remarrying. Perhaps she relished the independence and freedom of action that a widow, as opposed to a wife, enjoyed; perhaps she was devoted to the memory of her late husband. Perhaps she simply regarded her life as a full one without a second marriage. She had, after all, five children to concern herself with.

Naturally, Margaret's children soon felt the effect of their mother's restoration as well. For Henry Pole, Margaret's heir, there was suddenly the prospect of inheriting an earldom instead of some middling estates; for all (save for Reginald, whose career lay with the Church), their marital prospects were drastically improved.

As we have seen, Henry Pole attended Katherine of Aragon at her coronation and presumably remained at court, for he repeatedly received gifts of fine clothing from the royal purse: a gown of French tawny in November 1509, a gown of tawny velvet in November 1510, a gown of black velvet in May 1511, a black damask gown in November 1511, and another black velvet gown in May 1512, at which time he was named as one of the king's 'sewers' – that is, someone who would see to it that the king was properly served at table.[23] In July 1513, Henry Pole, having reached his majority, received livery of his father's lands.[24] These included what Henry Pole would make his principal residence: Bockmer, part of the manor of Medmenham in Buckinghamshire. When Henry VIII set off on his first French campaign in 1513, capturing Tournai, Henry Pole accompanied him, and came back knighted as Sir Henry Pole. From 1514, however, Sir Henry was known as Lord Montagu, apparently a courtesy title as he would not be summoned to Parliament until 1529.[25]

Lord Montagu's next step was to marry. His bride, whom he married no later than March 1519, when she is recorded as receiving a gift, and probably around 1517, judging from the 1532 marriage of their eldest child, was Jane Neville, daughter of George Neville, Lord Bergavenny. Margaret negotiated the financial arrangements concerning jointure and inheritance, as well as for the wedding itself, which in draft form included the provision that she and Bergavenny were to pay for their respective child's apparel and split the cost of the marriage licence and of the meat and drink at the wedding feast.[26] The couple were to have one son, naturally named Henry for the king (and coincidentally, for Montagu himself), and two daughters, Catherine and Winifred. Montagu's marriage did not distance him from his mother; he often dined with her and had rooms set aside for his use at her various residences. Indeed, Reginald Pole's secretary would describe him as 'the chief stay of his family'.[27]

Arthur Pole, Margaret's second son, began his court career in 1514 as part of the entourage accompanying Henry VIII's sister Mary to France for her marriage to Louis XII. (Also among Mary's attendants was, famously, one 'Mademoiselle Boleyn'.) The marriage, which took place on 9 October, did not survive the year, for Louis died on 31 December. Mary soon found consolation with the king's friend Charles Brandon, and the newlyweds and those attendants who had not already come home returned to England. Like Brandon, Arthur Pole shone on the jousting field, making his debut in 1516, the same year he was appointed a squire of the king's body. In 1518, he was made a gentleman of the Privy Chamber – a prized position, as such men were hand-picked by the king and enjoyed his trust and friendship. Arthur married a widowed heiress, Jane Pickering, the daughter of Sir Roger Lewknor, between 1519 and 1522, and fathered three children, (yet another) Henry, Mary and Margaret.[28]

Geoffrey, the youngest and ultimately most troublesome of Margaret's children, made little impression upon the historical record until the late 1520s. By July 1525, he had married Constance Pakenham, who in 1528 inherited the manor of Lordington in Sussex from her father, Sir Edmund Pakenham. The couple would have ten children. Geoffrey was knighted after 3 November 1529.[29]

Ursula, Margaret's only surviving daughter, received a gift of clothing from the king on 13 November 1513. On 16 February 1519, she married Henry Stafford, the heir to Edward Stafford, Duke of Buckingham – a marriage that should have in time made her the wife of the nation's leading peer. With this in mind, Buckingham, who had previously rejected Ursula as a match for his son in hopes of securing the Earl of Shrewsbury's daughter, demanded a dowry of 3,000 marks, increased to 4,000 marks if the king gave Margaret certain lands, which Margaret agreed to pay in instalments. In exchange, Buckingham was to settle lands worth £500 upon Ursula. Except for the bride's clothes, for which Margaret paid, Buckingham bore the expenses of the wedding. Henry Stafford was not yet eighteen at the time; because of his youth, he continued to live in his father's household with his new bride, who bore her first child (of fourteen, seven boys and seven girls) in November 1520.[30]

The most famous of Margaret's children, Reginald, continued in the path of the Church. In around 1512, he went to Oxford's Magdalen College, where he remained until around 1519, receiving his BA in 1515. In 1518, while Reginald was still at Oxford, the king conferred upon him the deanery of Wimborne Minster and the prebend of Ruscombe Southbury. Having paid him a pension during his stay at Oxford, the king in 1521 sent Reginald to study at Padua.[31]

Thus, as the second decade of the sixteenth century drew to a close, all looked bright for Margaret and her children. Meanwhile, Henry VIII had his own child's rearing to consider.

5

LADY GOVERNESS

From the very beginning, Margaret was to play an important role in the life of Mary, Katherine of Aragon's only child to survive infancy. (A son had lived only a couple of months; since then, the queen had experienced a series of miscarriages and a stillbirth.) Born at Greenwich Palace on 18 February 1516, Mary was christened two days later at the nearby Church of Friars Observant. In accordance with custom, Mary had three godparents at the font, two of her own gender and one of the opposite sex: Katherine, Countess of Devon, the last surviving of Edward IV's daughters; Agnes, Duchess of Norfolk; and Cardinal Wolsey. Immediately after the christening, Mary was confirmed, which required a third godmother: Margaret. The ceremony, though certainly not as grand as what would have been accorded a boy, was still impressive:

> From the court gate to the church door of the Friars was railed and hung with arras; the way being well gravelled and strewed with rushes. At the church door was set a house well framed of timber, covered with arras, where the Princess, with her godfather and godmother, abode. There she received her name Mary. Then they entered the church, which was hung with cloth of needlework garnished with precious stones and pearls. She was preceded by a goodly sight of gentlemen

and lords. Then followed the basin, borne by my Lord of Devonshire, supported by Lord Herbert; the taper by the Earl of Surrey, the salt by the Marquis of Dorset, Lady Dorset bearing the chrism. The Lord Chamberlain followed, with the Lord Steward on his right. Then the canopy, borne by Sir David Owen, Sir Nich. Vaux, Sir Thos. Aparre, and Sir Thomas Boleyn, under which was the Princess, borne by the Countess of Surrey. The Princess was assisted by the Duke of Norfolk at the head, and the Duke of Suffolk at the feet. Next, the Lady Katharine, the Duchess of Norfolk, &c. The Lord Cardinal, godfather, Lady Katharine and the Duchess of Norfolk, godmothers, at the font. The Countess of Salisbury at the bishopping. Then Te Deum sung by the King's chaplain.[1]

Mary was initially assigned to the care of a lady mistress, Lady Margaret Bryan, and a wet nurse, Katharine Pole (not Margaret's granddaughter, but the wife of Leonard Pole). As it became clear that Mary was unlikely to have a brother, however, her household began to assume the form of a royal heir's, with a household of greater size and status. Accordingly, by 1 May 1520, and most likely before that, Henry VIII appointed the Countess of Salisbury as Mary's governess, probably at the urging of the queen. Reginald Pole later claimed that Katherine of Aragon, not wishing simply to order Margaret to assume her post, had gone in person to Margaret's house 'together with the king and implore her to take up the burden willingly'.[2]

Margaret was at her new post in late May 1520, when much of the court set out for France for the meeting between Henry VIII and King Francis known as the Field of the Cloth of Gold. Although Margaret's new duties kept her in England, her sons Lord Montagu and Arthur were among the courtiers travelling to France. During the requisite tournaments, which began in June, Montagu and Arthur jousted on the team led by Henry Courtenay, Earl of Devon (soon to be Marquess of Exeter), who was their cousin as well as the king's. The team dressed in blue and white, with the blue side showing a woman's hand using a water can on a man's burning heart and the white side bearing the words *pour reveiller* ('to awake'). Arthur's performance earned him one of the prizes.[3]

Meanwhile, King Francis, whose son was betrothed to four-year-old Mary, had become suspicious when King Henry failed to bring his daughter to France. Concerned that the child might have some undisclosed defect, Francis sent envoys to England to have a look at his prospective daughter-in-law. Cardinal Wolsey notified the Privy Council in England of their impending arrival. Duly warned, the Countess of Salisbury and her staff, not to mention the little princess herself, rose to the occasion, as the Privy Council triumphantly reported to the king:

... [the] gentlemen of France of whose coming and entertainment we had advertisement by my lord Cardinal ... being well accompanied by the Lord Darcy and others repaired to your dearest daughter the [princess] at Richmond where they found her grace right honourable [and well] accompanied with your council and other lords both spiritual and temporal and her house and chambers right well appointed and furnished with a goodly company of gentlemen and tall yeomen. And as unto ladies there were in the chamber of presence attending on her grace besides the lady governess and other her gentlewomen the Duchess of Norfolk with her three daughters, the lady Margaret wife to the Lord Herbert Countess of Worcester, the ladies Gray and Neville, the lord John's wife, and sundry other ladies and gentlewomen and in the great chamber were many goodly gentlewomen well apparelled. And at the coming of the said gentlemen of France to the princess's presence her grace in such wise showed herself unto them first in welcoming and entertaining of them with most goodly countenance, proper communication, and pleasant pastime in playing at the virginals that they greatly marvelled and rejoiced the same her young and tender age considered. And soon after they departed again to London.

For their 'goodly cheer', Mary's household offered the envoys 'strawberries, wafers, wine, and hippocras in plenty'.[4]

At the Field of the Cloth of Gold, the Duke of Buckingham had made a fine show, having brought five chaplains, ten gentlemen, fifty-five servants and thirty horses overseas with him.[5] Probably he had done well sartorially too, as in 1513 when he had appeared at a previous excursion to France in apparel 'full of antelopes and swans of fine gold bullion and full of spangles, and little bells of gold, marvellous costly and pleasant to behold'.[6] The son of Henry Stafford, Duke of Buckingham, and Katherine Woodville, the youngest sister of Edward IV's queen, the younger Buckingham had been but five years old when his father, who had helped Richard III to the throne and then rebelled against him, paid the price for his treason on the scaffold in 1483. Unlike Margaret, who had felt the effects of her father's and her brother's execution for decades, Buckingham's loss of rank and status lasted for only two years; when Henry Tudor took the throne, he restored the boy to his title and to his immense landholdings, granting his wardship to Margaret Beaufort.

Yet Buckingham's rank, wealth and own royal blood (he was descended from Edward III through a couple of lines), not to mention his prickly personality, had made for uneasy relations with Henry VIII. He had no use for Henry's chief minister, Wolsey, or for the king's rapprochement with the French, and his relations with some of his own servants were fraught. All of this came to a head when, in April 1521, the duke was arrested for treason. After a trial, at which much of the evidence was provided by Buckingham's servants, he was executed on 17 May 1521. Buckingham probably had no intent to force Henry off his throne, but his musings on the possibility of his being the king's heir if the sonless Henry were to die, testimony that he had reminisced about his own father's alleged plan to kill Richard III with a dagger and his vocal displeasure with the king's policies sealed his fate.

Although Buckingham had lacked the common touch, he had been on good terms with Margaret and her children, and this connection was to prove costly. On 7 May, Sir William Fitzwalter reported that Henry Pole, Lord Montagu, had been arrested, along with his father-in-law, Lord Bergavenny. As for Arthur Pole, he was expelled from court, having reportedly asked Lord Leonard Grey to 'write concerning the imprisonment of the duke'; although exactly what Grey was supposed to write, much less to whom, went unreported by the source for this information, a Richard Pace. Pace also added that 'concerning the lady Salisbury the matter is under debate because of her nobility and goodness'.[7] Whatever the meaning of this murky statement, Margaret was clearly tainted by her connection with the doomed duke, for she lost her position in Mary's household.

There seems to have been little justification for the Pole family's disfavour other than guilt by association. It probably did not help, though, that Buckingham was reported to have said, in reference to the fate of Margaret's brother Warwick, 'God would punish it, by not suffering the King's issue to prosper, as appeared by the death of his son; and that his daughters prosper not, and that he had no issue male' – a matter that was to increasingly trouble the king as well as Buckingham.[8]

Nonetheless, the king's displeasure would be short-lived. Lord Montagu was soon released from prison, and the following May was chosen as one of the king's attendants for his meeting with Charles V at Canterbury. Both Lord Montagu and Arthur joined the king's 1523 French campaign, and it was there that Charles Brandon, Duke of Suffolk, knighted Arthur. By the New Year of 1522, Margaret herself had recovered enough royal favour for the queen to give her a gold pax that had in turn been given to the queen by the Countess of Devon.[9]

The member of the Pole family who suffered most from Buckingham's downfall was the duke's daughter-in-law, Ursula Stafford. Although Buckingham had been troubled by debt (a bane of many a nobleman's existence), he had lived luxuriously. Ursula and her husband had fully enjoyed this lifestyle as shown in the inventory's description of their clothing: gowns of cloth of gold, damask, satin and velvet; shoes of black velvet and leather;

a christening gown of blue velvet, furred and powdered with ermine; a counterpane showing a king and a woman in a green gown with a child in her arms; a counterpane depicting the Three Kings of Cologne; a tester of a bishop marrying a king and queen; cushions of green velvet and cloth of gold; and a leather chair covered with embroidery.[10] Buckingham's execution and attainder had left the young couple and their steadily growing family with nothing. Fortunately, the king in September 1522 granted them some of Buckingham's forfeited estates, but the Staffords were never again to live in the grand style to which they had become accustomed.

Four years after Buckingham's execution, Margaret reached her pinnacle of royal favour. King Henry, faced with the unlikelihood of having a legitimate heir, had been considering how best to deploy the two children he did have: Mary and an illegitimate son, Henry Fitzroy. In June 1525, Henry made his son the Duke of Richmond and Somerset and sent the small boy and a large household to Sheriff Hutton Castle, where the new duke would serve as the head of the King's Council of the North. Such unusual treatment – no royal bastard had been raised to the peerage since the twelfth century – naturally fuelled speculation that Henry might be planning to legitimatise Richmond at the expense of his legitimate half-sister.

But Henry had his own plans for Mary. Just two months after establishing Richmond in the North, Henry sent Mary to the Welsh Marches, where the nine-year-old princess was to preside over the Council of Wales and the Marches. If not an explicit admission that Mary was to be Henry's heir, it certainly sent that message: both Edward IV and Henry VII had sent their heirs, the ill-fated Edward V and Prince Arthur, to reside in the Marches once they passed through the earliest stages of childhood. Presiding over the princess's household of over 300 servants would be Margaret, alongside Mary's steward, Lord Ferrers, and her chamberlain, Lord Dudley. With expenses totalling nearly £4,500 per year, Mary's household was a splendid one.[11]

As Edward IV had done when sending his heir to Wales, Henry VIII set out a detailed set of instructions regulating his daughter's household at Ludlow. Margaret had the daunting task of overseeing 'all such things as concern the person of the said princess, her noble education and training in all virtuous demeanour'. The women around the princess were to 'use themselves sadly [decorously], honourably, virtuously and discreetly in words, countenance, gesture, behaviour and deed with humility, reverence, lowliness ... so as of them proceed no manner of example of evil or unfitting manner or conditions, but rather of good and godly behaviour'. No detail of the young princess's day-to-day routine was left to chance. Mary was to learn Latin and French, to practice on her virginals and other musical instruments, to dance, to take exercise in the open air and eat meat that was 'pure, well-prepared, dressed and served, with comfortable, joyous, and merry communication in all honourable and virtuous manner'.

Our view of Mary is indelibly coloured by her grim adolescence, when she was caught between warring parents, by the burnings of over 300 Protestants during her reign as queen and by her sad last years, during which she suffered two false pregnancies and pined for an absent husband who took only a polite interest in her. As a nine-year-old, however, she was lively, intelligent and attractive, with an apparent gift for courtly banter. Giles Duwes, Mary's former French tutor, writing after the household had disbanded, remembered an incident when Mary, following the tradition of drawing Valentines, picked the name of her gout-stricken treasurer, Sir Ralph Egerton. Young Mary referred to the older man as her 'husband adoptive' and scolded him for taking better care of his gout than he did of his wife (i.e., Mary herself). She then requested that Egerton teach her the full definition of love. In another incident recounted by Duwes, Mary scolded her almoner for not joining the household at dinner, reminding him that incidentally that she had praised his French and that he had assured her 'within a year I should speak as good or better than you'.[12]

After the near-family disaster stemming from Buckingham's execution, Margaret must have basked in her restoration to royal favour. She was on the best of terms with Katherine of Aragon, who in a letter to Mary wrote, '[I]t shall be a great comfort to me to see You keep your Latin and fair writing and all. And so I pray you to recommend me to my Lady of Salisbury.'[13] Margaret kept up cordial relations with the king as well: in January 1526, she gave him a New Year's gift of cambric, a fine cloth.[14]

Constance Pole, who was married to Margaret's son Geoffrey, and Catherine Pole, Lord Montagu's daughter, were also prominent in Mary's household, and doubtless had been placed there through Margaret's influence. Her position allowed her to influence other matters as well, as we see in this August 1527 letter to Anne Rede:

> I recommend me unto you, doing you to understand that I have received your letters by your servant concerning the marriage of your daughter, by the which I do perceive that the gentlewoman, being accompanied with your said daughter unto your house, hath informed you that it was my mind for her to certify you that the comptroller of the princess's household doth bear his singular favour to your said daughter. Truly she misused herself in giving you any such knowledge on my behalf, for I assure you that I did give unto her no commandment so to do; for at that time I had heard no communication touching that matter. Howbeit, since our departing from Hartlebury, the said comptroller hath moved and communed with me therein, of the which I have certified your daughter; but I can perceive nothing in her whereby any effect should be had or taken in that matter. Wherefore I pray you to be a good and natural mother unto her, and I doubt not but she will always use herself to you as a natural child ought to do to her mother; and would advise you to look well upon the matter which I sent you word of beforetime, that it may be brought to a good end, for in my mind it would be a very meet bargain if it be well finished and come to pass. And thus I pray God it may be accomplished to both your comforts.
> From Worcester, the 20th day of August.
>
> Margaret Salisbury[15]

The marriage, to Sir Giles Grevill, did eventually take place, though whether the countess's exertions brought it about we do not know.[16]

Sometime during this period, Margaret's second son, Arthur, died. He is last mentioned in the records on 20 March 1527, as part of an assessment of the members of the king's chamber,[17] but the date and cause of his death is not recorded. His death occurred before 1 August 1532, the date his widow, Jane Lewknor, entered into a marriage settlement with her third husband, William Barentyne.[18] It is quite possible, as Hazel Pierce has suggested, that Arthur fell victim to the sweating sickness, a deadly disease that struck England in 1528, carrying off William Compton, a favourite courtier of the king's, and sickening but ultimately sparing Anne Boleyn, with far-reaching consequences. Margaret was said to have made her will in 1528, an act which could have been necessitated by her son's death. Moreover, one of Arthur's children appears to have died around the same time as Arthur, according to Jane Lewknor, who complained that Lord Montagu had pressured her into taking a vow of chastity after Arthur's death 'when she was in extreme grief for the death of her husband Sir Arthur and one of her children'. He was buried at Bisham Abbey.[19]

Margaret certainly must have grieved for her second son, but nothing records her reaction to his death. If Arthur's death did occur during the 1528 sweating sickness epidemic, it did not prevent Margaret from taking advantage of that of his fellow courtier, William Compton. Since being restored to her Salisbury lands, Margaret had claimed ownership of the manors of Canford in Dorset, Ware in Hertfordshire, the Wyke in Middlesex, Deeping in Lincoln, Charton and Henstridge in Somerset and Aldebury, Trowbridge, Crombridge and Winterbourne in Wiltshire. Another person, however, claimed ownership of the manors, and he was a most powerful opponent: Henry VIII himself.[20]

The countess's doggedness in defending her claim against the king's illuminates an overlooked aspect of her character – particularly since, as Hazel Pierce, who has analysed the circumstances of this dispute in depth, points out, the king actually had the better claim to the land, although both were lacking in certain respects. It was apparently owing to the efforts of William Compton, who was the steward of some of these lands, that the king had been alerted to the flaws in Margaret's titles. In 1525, he granted Winterbourne to Katherine of Aragon and gave Canford and Deeping to Henry Fitzroy, Duke of Richmond, his illegitimate son. With Compton's death in 1528, however, Margaret seized the chance to renew the dispute. One of Margaret's councillors wrote the following plea on Margaret's behalf, abstracted as follows:

His very good lady, my lady of Salisbury, is sued for an obligation of 5,000 marks, in which she stands bound to the King, though she is probably not aware of it. As her charge of attending on the Princess keeps her at a distance from the King so that she cannot sue in person, those about her do not like to trouble her. Requests his correspondent to move the King for her. Her counsel say the 5,000 marks were given by her to the King after the lands of the earldom of Salisbury were restored to her. Of these the lordship of Canford and other lordships, to the value of 500 marks a year, were parcel, and she took the profits until the late Sir Will. Compton, 'for that he obtained not his purpose of her in marriage according to his suit,' surmised to the King that they belonged to the dukedom of Somerset. On this she was commanded by my lord Cardinal 'to amove her possession' till her right could be tried; which matter is still undetermined, though her counsel are clear as to her right. The 5,000 marks were granted by her to the King of her own free will, in the belief that he meant her to enjoy those lands, and 1,000l. were paid to my lord Cardinal. Hopes he will get Wolsey to stay the suit till the question of the title is determined.[21]

The extraordinary claim that Compton misrepresented the ownership of the lands in revenge for Margaret's refusing his proposal to her cannot be substantiated, although Compton, who was about a decade younger than Margaret, would have neither been the first nor the last knight to land a widowed noblewoman as a bride. Any proposal would have taken place before May 1512, when Compton married Werburga Cheyney.[22] Whatever its truth, the claim apparently failed to move the king, as Margaret never recovered the lands she believed were hers.

Meanwhile, in the summer of 1528, Mary and her household left the Marches – for good, as it turned out, although the move at the time may not have been regarded as a permanent one.[23] The princess spent the Christmases of 1529 and 1530 at court and otherwise lived in her household close to that of her parents, as noted by Milanese envoy Augustino Scarpinello, who wrote, 'The Lady Princess is always apart, at a distance of 10 or 15 miles, with a suitable establishment, and is heard to be already advanced in wisdom and stature.'[24] By Christmas of 1530, yet another noble cousin joined the household: Margaret Douglas, daughter of Henry VIII's sister Margaret and her second husband, Archibald Douglas, Earl of Angus.[25] Wilful and high-spirited, Margaret Douglas, who turned fifteen in October 1530, was just a few months older than the princess, and the two young women must have made for a lively, but challenging household for the countess to supervise.

There was a personal matter for Margaret to attend to as well: the marriage of her granddaughter, Catherine Pole, to Francis, Lord Hastings. The eldest son of George, Earl of Huntingdon, and Anne Stafford (sister to the Duke of Buckingham executed in 1521), Francis was around eighteen in 1531, when marital negotiations opened between Huntingdon on the one hand and Margaret and Montagu on the other. Margaret was to pay for Catherine's wedding finery and for half of the food and drink over three days of wedding festivities. More important, of course, was the land that the couple was to receive: 200 marks' worth immediately after the wedding, with the reversion of other manors and a jointure of 650 marks. When they wed in 1532, Catherine and Francis would be starting their married life with lands worth a total of £900, with the prospect of inheriting lands in Leicester, Yorkshire, Buckingham, Wiltshire, Somerset, Devon and Cornwall.[26] Both

Lord Montagu and Margaret were solicitous of the young couple: when Francis fell ill in April 1524, Lord Montagu stayed at the Garter ceremonies just long enough to perform his ceremonial role of bearing the sword before the king, after which 'he rode straight unbeware to anybody into Leicestershire to my said Lord of Hastings, where he remaineth yet, though the said young lord be past danger'.[27] Two years later, Hastings was again ailing, this time with a fever, which Lord Montagu informed Lord Lisle kept Margaret away from her house at Warblington.[28]

Mario Savorgnano, a Venetian visitor, paid a call upon Mary's household in August 1531, leaving us not only with a description of the princess, but of the Countess of Salisbury, her governess, as well. He wrote:

> We next went to another palace, called Richmond, where the Princess, her daughter, resides; and having asked the maggiordomo for permission to see her, he spoke to the chamberlain, and then to the governess, and they made us wait. Then after seeing the palace we returned into a hall, and having entered a spacious chamber where there were some venerable old men with whom we discoursed, the Princess came forth accompanied by a noble lady advanced in years, who is her governess, and by six maids of honour. We kissed her hand, and she asked us how long we had been in England, and if we had seen their Majesties, her father and mother, and what we thought of the country; she then turned to her attendants, desiring them to treat us well, and withdrew into her chamber. This Princess is not very tall, has a pretty face, and is well proportioned with a very beautiful complexion, and is 15 years old. She speaks Spanish, French, and Latin, besides her own mother-English tongue, is well grounded in Greek, and understands Italian, but does not venture to speak it. She sings excellently, and plays on several instruments, so that she combines every accomplishment. We were then taken to a sumptuous repast, after which we returned to our

lodging, whither, according to the fashion of the country, the Princess sent us a present of wine and ale (which last is another beverage of theirs), and white bread.[29]

Savorgnano's description of the attractive, courteous and well-educated Mary did credit to both the countess and her charge. But all was not well in the well-run and hospitable household. It had not been for some time.

6

PERSEVERANCE

If one woman in English history needs no introduction, it is Anne Boleyn. The collision of Henry VIII's increasingly desperate desire for a male heir and his infatuation with the commoner and her beautiful dark eyes would wreak havoc, with a devastating effect upon Mary's household and all of those connected with it.

Henry's marriage to Katherine of Aragon had started to teeter well before Anne glided onto the scene, however. Early in the marriage, in January 1510, Katherine had miscarried a daughter; the following New Year, she delighted her husband by bringing forth a son. But the royal boy, Henry, died just six weeks later. Two more ill-fated births followed in 1513 and 1514, of sons who were either stillborn or died soon after delivery. This grim procession was broken by Mary's birth in 1516, only to be followed by another stillbirth in November 1518. Katherine, who was nearly thirty-three at the time, would not give birth again.[1]

As Katherine turned increasingly to religion and to the rearing of her only surviving child, Henry indulged himself elsewhere. His early flings may not have gone further than the sport of courtly love, although there is a possibility that Henry had a full-fledged affair with a Frenchwoman named Jane Poppincourt, who left England in 1516 with an exceedingly generous gift of £100 from the king.[2] There is no doubt about Henry's next dalliance, this one with a young lady named Elizabeth 'Bessie' Blount, for in the summer of 1519 it bore fruit in the shape of a healthy boy, who was named Henry Fitzroy after his delighted father. Bessie was soon given a husband, Gilbert Tailboys, a perfectly respectable send-off for a royal mistress, and Henry moved on to another amour, Mary Boleyn, whose father, Thomas Boleyn, had long served the Crown.

With Katherine of Aragon's childbearing years behind her, and her once winsome looks having faded as well – one Venetian described her as 'rather ugly' in 1515, while another, more gallant Venetian could manage only a polite 'not handsome' in 1519 – the queen and the king had settled into a respectful, but increasingly separate and probably sexless, relationship by the 1520s.[3] This chilly state of affairs took a considerable turn for the worse in 1525, when Katherine's nephew, Emperor Charles V, who had been betrothed to Princess Mary, abandoned the match in favour of a marriage with Isabella of Portugal, who had two overwhelming advantages over Mary: she could bring Charles a huge dowry, and she was of childbearing age. Henry, of course, did not share Charles' appreciation for the advantages of the Portuguese match, and historian R. B. Wernham has suggested that it was this which led Henry to begin the process of casting off those ties with Katherine and her native Spain. It was soon after this that Henry ennobled the illegitimate Henry Fitzroy and set him up in his household in the north, to the dismay of the queen.[4] But what was percolating in Henry's mind by the mid-1520s was far worse than Katherine suspected: the king had begun to question the very validity of his marriage. Why had his queen failed to provide him with a surviving male heir? Modern medicine could have supplied any number of answers to this question, but without the benefit of such knowledge, Henry, who was genuinely interested in theology in any case, had to search for a divine answer to his question. It soon presented itself: he had married his brother's wife, an act prohibited by the Book of Leviticus, which admonished, 'You shall not uncover the nakedness of your brother's wife: because it is the nakedness of your brother' (18:16) and 'If a man shall take his brother's wife, it is an unclean thing: he has uncovered his brother's nakedness. They shall be childless' (20:21). The Book of

Deuteronomy offered a contradictory view, which in fact not only justified Henry's marriage to Katherine but mandated it – 'When brothers live together, and one of them dies without children, the wife of the deceased shall not marry to another: but his brother shall take her, and raise up seed for his brother' (20:6). The facts that his marriage had not actually been childless and that he had obtained a papal dispensation for it were also awkward. But Henry, having staked his claim on Leviticus, would never back down from it.

Precisely when the king decided that his marriage was invalid is unknown. Equally elusive is the point at which Henry began to consider a specific replacement for his queen. She was nearer at hand, however, than anyone – including the principals – realised.

Anne Boleyn was one of the three surviving children of a favoured courtier, Sir Thomas Boleyn, and Elizabeth Howard, whose father, Thomas Howard, was the 2nd Duke of Norfolk. She was a bright girl, and Sir Thomas, whose especially fluent French served him well as a diplomat, seized upon this and his international connections to place his daughter in the sophisticated court of Margaret of Austria. The marriage of Mary, Henry VIII's younger sister, to King Louis XII of France meant that Anne was summoned to France to attend the new queen. Louis had little time to enjoy his young bride, however, for he died after just weeks of marriage. Having shocked both the French and the English by marrying King Henry's close friend Charles Brandon, Duke of Suffolk, Mary returned with her new husband to England. Anne, however, did not follow. Instead, she joined the household of the new French queen, Francis I's bride Claude, where she remained for some time before returning to England. Thoroughly Frenchified, and possessed of considerable charisma, she made a splash at court, where in 1522 she made her debut at a pageant in the extremely apt role of Perseverance. By 1526 she had caught the royal eye, though Henry's initial efforts were directed toward making her his mistress (a role Anne's sister, Mary, had filled for a time), as shown in the series of extraordinary love letters that survive from the king to his subject. 'If it shall please you to do me the office of a true loyal mistress and friend and to give yourself up, body and soul to me,' Henry declared, 'I promise you that not only shall the name be given you, but that also I will take you for my only mistress, rejecting from thought and affection all others save yourself, to serve you only.'[5]

The first salvo in Henry's campaign to free himself from his marriage came in May 1527, when Henry's mainstay and Archbishop of York, Thomas Wolsey, called Henry before him to answer for having unlawfully married his brother's widow. Henry, clearly the impetus behind this, dutifully made an appearance, but the proceedings (of which Katherine of Aragon was not informed) ultimately went nowhere. Troubled, perhaps, by the prospect of taking the drastic step of single-handedly declaring the king's marriage invalid, Wolsey (and, perhaps, his royal master) decided to adjourn the proceedings in order to consult with theologians. Matters were further complicated by the sack of Rome, which had left the Pope a prisoner in the hands of Katherine of Aragon's nephew, Emperor Charles. Instead, Wolsey set off to France, in hopes of being elected papal deputy, while Henry took upon himself the disagreeable task of telling his queen that her services were no longer needed. As reported by the imperial ambassador, Inigo Mendoza:

No intimation or summons had up to that date been made to the Queen, but since then, on the 22nd of last month [June], the King has virtually separated himself from the Queen, telling her that they had been in mortal sin during all the years they had lived together, and that this being the opinion of many canonists and theologians whom he had consulted on the subject, he had come to the resolution, as his conscience was much troubled thereby, to separate himself from her mensâ et thoro, and wished her to choose the place to which she would retire. The Queen bursting into tears, and being too much agitated to reply, the King said to her, by way of consolation, that all should be done for the best and begged her to keep secrecy upon what he had told her. This the King must have said, as it is generally believed, to inspire her with confidence and prevent her from seeking the redress she is entitled to by right, and also to keep the intelligence from the public, for so great is the attachment that the English bear to the Queen that some demonstration would probably take place in her household. Not that the people of England are ignorant of the King's intentions, for the affair is as notorious as if it had been proclaimed by the public crier, but they cannot believe that he will ever carry so wicked a purpose into effect.[6]

As Mendoza noted, finding that the king's marriage was invalid would in effect render Mary illegitimate, putting her on the same footing as Henry Fitzroy. As Katherine of Aragon's close friend and Mary's governess, Margaret must have been dismayed and disgusted by this shocking news, but her reaction is not recorded.

Ferdinand and Isabella's daughter, however, was not one to quietly accept the destruction of her marriage. As Wolsey reported to the king on 1 July, she was 'very stiff and obstinate', and insisted that Arthur 'did never know her carnally' – that is, that her short-lived marriage had never been consummated and thus would not serve as an impediment to her marrying Henry.[7] Coolly disregarding the king's request for secrecy, she employed a stratagem to send one of her servants, Francisco Felipez, to inform Emperor Charles of her plight. Charles responded promptly, writing in July 1527 to Katherine, Henry, and the Pope, and promising not to 'desert the Queen, our good aunt, in her troubles'.[8]

Meanwhile, the relationship between Henry and Anne was soon to take a new turn, for as the imperial ambassador reported on 16 August 1527, 'It is generally believed that if the King can obtain a divorce he will end by marrying a daughter of Master [Boleyn].'[9] That same month, Henry sent William Knight to Rome with an application for a papal dispensation that allowed the king to take a new wife. The application requested permission for Henry to marry a woman with whose sister he had had sexual intercourse, as well as one who herself had slept with Henry. As the sister of Mary Boleyn, Henry's former mistress, Anne fell into the first category, and G. W. Bernard has suggested that Anne might have fallen into the second category as well, sleeping with the king until the pair deemed it prudent to abstain from intercourse while the delicate matter of dissolving Henry's existing marriage was going forward.[10] But regardless of whether Henry and Anne had consummated their relationship, they were in for a long wait to legalise it.

In June 1528, Pope Clement VII – no longer captive but very much in a delicate position vis-a-vis the emperor – ordered Cardinal Lorenzo Campeggio to judge Henry and Katherine's case. The ailing cardinal finally arrived in England in October. On 24 October, he and Cardinal Wolsey made a proposal to Katherine – that she enter a house of religion, a sensible enough solution given that Katherine was well past her childbearing years and that as envisioned by Campeggio, Mary would still retain her place in the succession behind any male heirs the king might have. The queen, however, was having none of this. As Campeggio gloomily reported, '[S]he assured me that she would never do so; that she intended to live and die in the estate of matrimony, into which God had called her, and that she should always be of that opinion, and would not change it. She repeated this many times so determinately and deliberately that I am convinced she will act accordingly. She insists that everything shall be decided by sentence, and if that should go against her, she would then remain as free as his Highness; saying, that neither the whole kingdom on the one hand, nor any great punishment on the other, although she might be torn limb from limb, should compel her to alter this opinion; and that if after death she should return to life, rather than change it, she would prefer to die over again.' He concluded, 'I assure you that from all her conversation and discourse I have always judged her to be a prudent lady, and now more so. But as she can, without prejudice, as I have said above, avoid such great perils and difficulties, her obstinacy in not accepting this sound counsel does not much please me.'[11]

Perhaps Katherine's intransigence was fuelled by the knowledge that she had public opinion on her side. As the chronicler Hall reported, '[T]he common people ... and in especial women & other that favoured the queen talked largely, and said that the king for his pleasure would take another wife.' In an attempt at damage control, Henry in November 1528 summoned a number of prominent men to Bridewell, where he praised Katherine as a woman possessing 'all good qualities appertaining to nobility', and declared that if his marriage was indeed valid, he would choose her 'above all other women'. Yet ignoring the doubts about his marriage's validity and his daughter's legitimacy would leave the nation vulnerable, upon his death, to a situation such as that which had arisen following the death of Edward IV. (Here Henry rather disingenuously ignored the fact that it had been he himself who raised the doubts about his marriage's validity.) The reception was less than overwhelming, as Hall reported: 'To see what contention was made amongst the hearers of this oration, it was a strange sight, for some sighed and said nothing, other were sorry to see the king so troubled in his conscience. Other that favoured the Queen much sorrowed that the matter was now opened, and so every man spake as his heart moved him.'[12]

At last, on 18 June 1529, following a series of legal manoeuvrings on both sides, the legatine court tasked with deciding the validity of Henry's marriage opened. The king's presence was not required, so he appeared via proxy, but Katherine took the opportunity to come in person to protest against the authority of the two cardinals, Wolsey and Campeggio, to hear the case – and to file an appeal asking that the matter be moved to London.[13] Three days later, both the king and queen appeared in the great chamber at Blackfriars. Though Wolsey's gentleman usher and biographer, George Cavendish, marvelled at the 'strange sight' of a king and queen appearing in court 'like common persons', there was nothing common about the couple who settled themselves in their respective places, the king on the right under a canopy of gold brocade, the queen on the left under another canopy.[14] After the king declared his intent to no longer live in mortal sin and begged the cardinals to resolve his case, Wolsey asked the king to assure the audience that Wolsey had not been the instigator of the divorce. Then, in one of the great set pieces of Tudor England, as described by Cavendish, the queen rose from her seat.

[B]ecause she could not come directly to the king for the distance which severed them, she took pain to go about unto the king, kneeling down at his feet in the sight of all the court and assembly, to whom she said in effect, in broken English, as followeth:

'Sir,' quoth she, 'I beseech you for all the loves that hath been between us, and for the love of God, let me have justice and right, take of me some pity and compassion, for I am a poor woman and a stranger born out of your dominion, I have here no assured friend, and much less indifferent counsel; I flee to you as to the head of justice within this realm. Alas! Sir, wherein have I offended you, or what occasion of displeasure have I designed against your will and pleasure? Intending (as I perceive) to put me from you, I take God and all the world to witness, that I have been to you a true humble and obedient wife, ever conformable to your will and pleasure, that never said or did anything to the contrary thereof, being always well pleased and contented with all things wherein ye had any delight or dalliance, whether it were in little or much, I never grudged in word or countenance, or showed a visage or spark of discontentation. I loved all those whom ye loved only for your sake, whether I had cause or no; and whether they were my friends or my enemies. This twenty years I have been your true wife or more, and by me ye have had divers children, although it hath pleased God to call them out of this world, which hath been no default in me.

'And when ye had me at the first, I take God to be my judge, I was a true maid without touch of man; and whether it be true or no, I put it to your conscience. If there be any just cause by the law that ye can allege against me, either of dishonesty or any other impediment to banish and put me from you, I am well content to depart, to my great shame and dishonour; and if there be none, then here I most lowly beseech you let me remain in my former estate, and receive justice at your princely hands. The king your father was in the time of his reign of such estimation through the world for his excellent wisdom, that he was accounted and called of all men the second Solomon; and my father Ferdinand, King of Spain, who was esteemed to be one of the wittiest princes that reigned in Spain many years before, were both wise and excellent kings in wisdom and princely behaviour. It is not therefore to be doubted, but that they elected and gathered as wise counsellors about them as to their high discretions was thought meet. Also, as me seemeth there was in those days as wise, as well-learned men, and men of as good judgment as be at this present in both realms, who thought then the marriage between you and me good and lawful. Therefore is it a wonder to me what new inventions are now invented against me, that never intended but honesty. And cause me to stand to the order and judgment of this new court, wherein ye may do me much wrong, if ye intend any cruelty; for ye may condemn me for lack of sufficient answer, having no indifferent counsel, but such as be assigned me, with whose wisdom and learning I am not acquainted. Ye must consider that they cannot be indifferent counsellors for my part which be your subjects, and taken out of your own council before, wherein they be made privy, and dare not, for your displeasure, disobey your will and intent, being once made privy thereto. Therefore I most humbly require you, in the way of charity, and for the love of God, who is the just judge, to spare the extremity of this new court, until I may be advertised what way and order my friends in Spain will advise me to take. And if ye will not extend to me so much indifferent favour, your pleasure then be fulfilled, and to God I commit my case!'

And even with that she rose up, making low courtesy to the king, and so departed from thence. Many supposed that she would have resorted again to her former place; but she took her direct way out of the house, leaning (as she was wont always to do) upon the arm of her General Receiver, called Master Griffith. And the king being advertised of her departure, commanded the crier to call her again, who called her by the name of 'Catherine Queen of England, come into the court, etc' With that quoth Master Griffith, 'Madam, ye be called again.' 'On, on,' quoth she, 'it maketh no matter, for it is no indifferent court for me, therefore I will not tarry: go on your ways.' And thus she departed out of that court, without any farther answer at that time, or at any other, nor would never appear at any other court after.

The French ambassador, Jean du Bellay, commented, 'If the matter was to be decided by women, he would lose the battle; for they did not fail to encourage the Queen at her entrance and departure by their cries, telling her to care for nothing, and other such words; while she recommended herself to their good prayers, and used other Spanish tricks.' Casually, he added that Katherine had filed an appeal to Rome, but that he did not think it a matter of importance.[15]

Although Katherine had absented herself from the court, two bishops, John Fisher, Bishop of Rochester, and John Clerk, Bishop of Bath and Wells, had been given the very unenviable task of representing her against the king. Bishop Fisher had been brought into the royal circle by Henry's paternal grandmother, Margaret, Countess of Richmond (who no doubt would have been appalled by her grandson's actions), and had delivered her eulogy. Appointed to the bishopric of Rochester by Henry VII, he had put his considerable talents to work during Henry VIII's reign by composing polemics against Lutheranism. But it was not for these treatises, but for the martyrdom he would achieve in defence of his queen, that he is best remembered today. His moment came on 28 June, when, as told by Campeggio's secretary, Bishop Fisher 'delivered an oration before the people to the Cardinals, the tenor of which was, that, having by virtue of the King's commission studied this cause between the King and the Queen, he had become positive that their marriage was holy and good, and could be dissolved only by God; that he was prepared to die for this truth; and that if he died for such a cause, he would not believe his death to be less [un]just than the execution of St. John the Baptist. He presented [to the Cardinals] a book composed by himself upon this case, for them to see. This event has given rise to much discussion; and as this man is a man of good fame, the King can no longer persist in dissolving the marriage; for this man being adverse to it, the kingdom will not permit the Queen to suffer wrong.'[16] The secretary's optimism would prove unfounded, but not the bishop's recognition that opposition to the king could prove fatal.

As it turned out, Katherine's dramatic appearance and Bishop Fisher's speech were the high points of the legatine court. Campeggio, who was by no means eager to issue a judgment, announced on 31 July that the court, following the Roman calendar, would be adjourned until October. As it was, it never met again, Katherine's appeal having succeeded.[17] Campeggio returned to Rome, while Wolsey, having failed to free Henry from his marriage, returned to disgrace and downfall. Forced to surrender the Great Seal in October, he was replaced as Lord Chancellor by Sir Thomas More, who himself had no desire to become entangled in what was called the king's Great Matter. The king, eager to make use of the talented More, agreed that only those 'whose consciences could well enough agree therein' would have to do with the Great Matter.[18]

Up to this point, Margaret and her children had been on the periphery of these events. Margaret could have hardly failed to deplore the king's treatment of his queen and his daughter, but she had apparently had the prudence to keep her thoughts to herself. Her sons, however, could not escape involvement.

The scholarly Reginald Pole was a natural for the king's cause. Having been sent to Padua by the king to study in 1521, Reginald had avoided the turmoil that had engulfed his family following Buckingham's execution. He had probably returned to England by 1527, at which point he was elected dean of Exeter Cathedral. He may have begun to learn Hebrew; it has been suggested that the king was grooming him to play a role in the Great Matter. Indeed, in October 1529 Henry sent Reginald to Paris as part of an effort to obtain from universities opinions favourable to his cause. Although Reginald would later maintain that he carried out this mission with the utmost reluctance, historian Thomas F. Mayer has questioned this, for he nonetheless was quick to remind the king of his hard work, which culminated in July 1529 when the theological faculty of the University of Paris issued their declaration in Henry's favour.[19] His mission accomplished, Reginald returned to England in the summer of 1530.

Margaret's eldest son, who in 1529 had taken his place in the House of Lords, was also doing his part to further the king's interest. In May 1530, Henry assembled members of the nobility and clergy at Westminster, where they were presented with a petition urging the Pope to grant Henry's longed-for divorce. Lord Montagu joined the rest in subscribing his signature and seal to the petition – described by J. J. Scarisbrick, with its multitude of seals of the good and the great, as 'physically, perhaps the most impressive piece uttered by Tudor England'. Geoffrey, Margaret's youngest son, though beginning to run dangerously into debt, also enjoyed royal favour during this time; between November 1529 and May 1530 he was knighted, and he sat in the parliament of 1529 as the member for Wilton.[20]

Cardinal Wolsey, meanwhile, had been banished to his home at Esher, after which the king vacillated between heaping him with humiliation and sending him tokens of his continuing favour. In the spring of 1530, he obeyed the king's order to relocate to his archdiocese of York, and he dutifully signed the papal petition of July 1530. Banished from court, Wolsey was a model bishop, washing the feet of poor men and confirming hundreds of children, but his enemies suspected that he was engineering his return to power and that he was secretly treating with foreign powers. The news that Pope Clement had drafted a bull (ultimately never issued) prohibiting Henry's remarriage while the Great Matter was still pending helped seal Wolsey's fate. Henry ordered the cardinal's arrest, which occurred on 4 November 1530. Sir William Kingston, the Constable of the Tower, went north to escort the disgraced cardinal to London, but whatever grim fate awaited Wolsey there was forestalled by his failing health. On 26 November, barely able to stay on his mule, he reached Leicester Abbey, where he died three days later, famously lamenting to Kingston, 'If I had served God as diligently as I have done the king, he would not have given me over in my grey hairs.' Wolsey was buried at Leicester

Abbey, which was subsequently dissolved and destroyed. Unlike the skeleton of Richard III, exhumed from the abbey site in 2012, Wolsey's remains have yet to be discovered.[21]

During this period, Henry and Katherine had publicly put on a show of cordial relations, even as the couple continued their legal manoeuvres. As Augustino Scarpinello reported in June 1530 to the Duke of Milan, 'The Queen also is with his Majesty, and they pay each other, reciprocally, the greatest possible attention, or compliments, in the Spanish fashion, with the utmost mental tranquillity, as if there had never been any dispute whatever between them; yet has the affair not slackened in the least, although at this present but little is being done here, as both parties are collecting votes, in France, Italy and several other places, but it is not yet known with what success. At any rate, this most virtuous Queen maintains strenuously, that all her King and Lord does, is done by him for true and pure conscience' sake, and not from any wanton appetite.'[22] Eustace Chapuys, who had recently taken over as imperial ambassador and who would become the queen's and Mary's ally, wrote to the Emperor Charles that same month, 'I wrote lately to Your Majesty that if the Lady [Anne] could only be kept away from Court for a little while, the Queen might still regain her influence over the King, for he does not seem to bear any ill-will towards her. Quite lately he sent her some cloth begging her to have it made into shirts for him. The Lady, hearing of this, sent for the person who had taken the cloth – one of the principal gentlemen of the bedchamber – and although the King himself confessed that the cloth had been taken to the Queen by his order, she abused the bearer in the King's very presence, threatening that she would have him punished severely.'[23]

The divorce proceedings, meanwhile, were taking on an increasingly farcical tone. In September 1530, Gregorio Casale, Henry's representative in Rome, confided to his master, 'A few days since the Pope secretly proposed to me the following condition; that your Majesty might be allowed to have two wives. I told him I could not undertake to make any such proposition, because I did not know whether it would satisfy your Majesty's conscience.' Evidently it did not. In a still lower point, in July 1531, Henry ordered another representative, William Benet, to stress that Arthur had been an oversexed royal who complained that he was not permitted to have intercourse with his wife as frequently as he desired, solicited other women for sex, and displayed his 'erect and inflamed member' as proof of his frustration.²⁴

That same month, the king and queen's odd relationship came to an end. On 14 July, when the royal couple and Anne Boleyn were all at Windsor, Henry and Anne left on a hunting trip without giving Katherine a chance to bid the king farewell. The two would never meet again. When Katherine inquired via messenger about the king's health, as was her custom, and expressed her regret about not having bid her husband farewell, the king sent her a rude reply. '[I]t was indifferent to him whether she sent to inquire after his health or not. She had hitherto caused him much annoyance and sorrow in a thousand ways.' There was one consolation for Katherine: Mary, and probably Margaret as well, was visiting her. That previous April, Mary had fallen ill with a stomach condition and had begged to be allowed to visit her parents. The king refused; Chapuys thought he did so to gratify the spite of Anne Boleyn.²⁵ Now that Anne and Henry's absence cleared the way for a visit between mother and daughter, Chapuys hoped that the pair would 'pass their time in sport and visiting the royal seats around Windsor'.²⁶ One hopes that they did spend their time pleasantly, for shortly before Mario Savorgnano's visit to Richmond in August, Henry ordered that Katherine and Mary go their separate ways: Katherine to The More in Hertfordshire, a former residence of Cardinal Wolsey, and Mary to Richmond.²⁷ It was, in fact, the last time mother and daughter would see each other, although for the time being they were spared that knowledge. Katherine's primary complaint was her lodgings, which she described as 'one of the worst in England'. If this was to last, she groused to Chapuys, 'she would much prefer and would be indeed happy to be sent as a prisoner to the Tower of London, for as her sufferings could not be greater than they are now, she might, were her misfortunes generally known, hope that everyone would pray God to arm her with patience, and inspire him (the King) with better sentiments'.²⁸

7

UNHEARD-OF CRUELTY

The year 1532 dawned miserably for Katherine and her allies, and cheerfully for Anne Boleyn. It started with a row over gift-giving. Breaking with custom, Henry refused to send the queen a New Year's gift and had ordered his courtiers to abstain as well; he had also left the queen's and the princess's ladies (including, presumably, Margaret) off his list. Nonetheless, Katherine, either unaware of the king's intentions or being deliberately provocative, sent the king a finely worked gold cup, which he refused. Lest Katherine, having had her gift returned to her, make an attempt to redeliver it in person with a gaggle of courtiers watching, Henry ordered that the cup not be returned until the evening. Anne Boleyn fared rather better. Having sent the king 'certain darts, worked in the Biscayan fashion, richly ornamented', she in turn received 'rich hangings for one room, and a bed covered with gold and silver cloth, crimson satin, and embroidery richer than all the rest'. Chapuys went on to add, 'The Lady [Anne], moreover, is still lodging where the Queen formerly was, and during the late festivities has been attended by almost the same number of the ladies as the Queen herself had formerly in her suite, as if she were already a Queen.' As the chronicler Hall summed it up, 'All men said there was no mirth in that Christmas because the queen and her ladies were absent.'[1]

That same month, Reginald Pole left England for what would turn out to be an absence of over twenty years.[2] Precisely why he left is murky, as Thomas Mayer has pointed out. Chapuys claimed that, unable to accept the king's planned divorce, Reginald had refused the archbishopric of York and, knowing that he would have to speak out against the divorce if the issue arose in Parliament, had requested permission to resume his studies abroad. Yet Henry's claimed reaction – immediately agreeing to his request, promising to continue his income of 400 ducats, and allowing him to retain his benefices – does not quite ring true, given that at this point in time Henry was not noted for his indulgence toward those who opposed his divorce. Moreover, Reginald did not have a place in Parliament from which to speak.

Pole does seem to have given the king his opinion on the marriage. Thomas Cranmer, writing to Anne Boleyn's father in 1531, claimed that Pole had 'written a book much contrary to the king his purpose' urging Henry to submit the question of the validity of his marriage to Katherine to the Pope.[3] In later years, Reginald was to claim, in accounts that varied slightly with each telling, that he had a stormy interview with the king, at a time which is not at all clear. Perhaps the safest guess is that Reginald had misgivings about the king's course of action, coupled with a preference for the scholarly life over that of a courtier, which impelled him to go abroad.

It was a wise decision, because in the midst of all of the petty quarrels over goodbyes and Christmas presents, momentous changes had been taking place. Unable to bend Rome to his will, Henry would break with Rome. In January 1531, the king took the bizarre, and brilliant, step of issuing a writ of praemunire against the entire English clergy for having recognised the traitorous Wolsey's authority as papal legate. At the Convocation, the nervous clerics agreed to pay a huge fine in return for a royal pardon, after which the victorious king had made another demand: that he be recognised as 'Supreme Head of the Church of England'. Convocation had done so, but added the proviso 'as far as the law of Christ allow[ed]' – which, of course, was open to a great deal of interpretation.

Thomas Cromwell, a lawyer and a former servant of Wolsey's whose talents had been identified by the king, had been instrumental in making these manoeuvres a success. In the spring of 1532 he delivered yet another victory for the king when he exploited the anti-clerical feelings of the Commons, which resulted on 18 March in the Commons delivering a 'Supplication against the Ordinaries' to the king, denouncing the operations of the ecclesiastical courts. Naturally, Henry approved of the supplication and sent it to Convocation, which in May responded with its 'Submission of the Clergy', which in effect gave the king the right to pass upon all legislation of the Church. Appalled, Thomas More promptly resigned as chancellor. Cromwell's triumph was followed in August by the death of William Warham, the octogenarian Archbishop of Canterbury. The man Henry chose for his replacement was yet another new talent: Thomas Cranmer, an academic at Cambridge with evangelical leanings who was responsible for the suggestion that Henry canvass European universities to gain their support for the Great Matter. Having produced translations for the king such as the revealingly titled *The determinations of the most famous and most excellent universities of Italy and France, that it is unlawful for a man to marry his brother's wife; that the pope hath no power to dispense therewith*, Cranmer had later been employed by the king as an ambassador. Henry's promotion of him was both surprising and distressing for Cranmer, who while abroad had ignored the Church's requirement that clergy be celibate and had taken a wife, Margaret. Leaving his wife behind in Germany (she would later secretly join his household in England), he took up his new position in January 1533.

Meanwhile, with the clergy subdued and a sympathetic Archbishop of Canterbury on the way, Henry and Anne were in high spirits. In September 1532, Henry VII created Anne Boleyn Marchioness (technically, Marquis) of Pembroke, thereby giving her noble status that made her more suitable as a prospective bride. Only one other woman in England held a noble title in her own right, that person being Margaret herself. What she felt about sharing this honour with a lady whom many regarded as a mere concubine can be surmised without a great deal of difficulty.

Fresh from this triumph, Henry and Anne began planning a trip to France to meet with King Francis. It would not do for Anne Boleyn to set off on this journey without proper jewels, and she wanted Katherine's. The invaluable Chapuys reported:

But though on this matter of the journey and interview the courtiers appear cold and indifferent, certain it is that the Lady [Anne] thinks otherwise, for knowing very well how to make hay while the sun shines, she has not been slack to provide herself with rich and most expensive dresses and ornaments, which the King has ordered to be bought for the occasion. After sending her his own jewels (baghes), the King has, I hear, lately given the duke of Norfolk commission, and he has come down here on purpose, to procure through a third person those belonging to the Queen; who, I am told, said to the bearer of the Royal message: 'I cannot present the King with my jewels as he desires, inasmuch as when, on a late occasion, I, according to the custom of this kingdom, presented him with a New Year's gift he warned me to refrain from such presents in future. Besides which (she said) it is very annoying and offensive to me, and I would consider it a sin and a load upon my conscience if I were persuaded to give up my jewels for such a wicked purpose as that of ornamenting a person who is the scandal of Christendom, and is bringing vituperation and infamy upon the King, through his taking her with him to such a meeting across the Channel. Yet,' continued the Queen, 'if the King sends expressly for my jewels I am ready to obey his commands in that as well as in all other matters'. Though highly displeased and sore at the Queen's answer the King nevertheless did send a gentleman of his chamber, who brought express orders to the Queen's

Chancellor, and to her Chamberlain, to see to the delivery of the said jewels besides a letter to the Queen herself in credence of the messenger, who said to her in the King's name that he was very much astonished at her not having sent her jewels forthwith when he first asked for them, as the queen of France, her sister, and many other [ladies] would have done. Upon which the Queen gently pleaded excuse for her former refusal, and sent him the whole of her jewels, and the King, as I am given to understand, is very much pleased and glad at it.[4]

In October 1532, Henry and a suitably bejewelled Anne set off on their voyage. Among the lovers' entourage of about 2,000 was Margaret's son Lord Montagu, who in turn had twenty men of his own in tow.[5] The trip was an unqualified success, for Anne and Henry consummated (or, if one accepts Barnard's view, rekindled) their relationship at some point during it, or at least soon afterward.[6]

Around 25 January 1533, or perhaps even earlier, Henry took Anne as his second wife, despite the inconvenient presence of a first wife.[7] Although Anne was soon flaunting her pregnancy around court, the wedding itself remained a secret for the time being while the details needed to push one queen aside and bring another forward were smoothed out. Cranmer was consecrated as bishop, and Parliament passed the Act of Appeals, which provided that ecclesiastical matters (including, of course, 'causes of matrimony and divorce') would no longer be appealed to Rome. Convocation voted that the Pope lacked the power to grant a dispensation allowing a man to marry the widow of his deceased brother.[8] Bishop Fisher, who had voted against the majority in Convocation, was arrested, as Chapuys surmised, for 'his having so manfully taken up the defence of the Pope and of the Queen', and given into the custody of Bishop Stephen Gardiner. There remained, however, the awkward business of telling Katherine of Aragon that she had been downgraded from queen to Dowager Princess of Wales and of her husband's nuptials, a task which fell to Charles Brandon, Duke of

Suffolk (the king's brother-in-law) and to Thomas Howard, Duke of Norfolk, along with two others. The quartet told Katherine 'that she need not trouble herself about returning to him, for he had already taken another wife, and that in future she must abstain from calling herself or being addressed as queen'. Having completed what must have been a very unpleasant mission, 'with much bowing and ceremony, and many excuses for having in obedience to the king's commands fulfilled so disagreeable a duty, the deputies withdrew'.[9]

These preliminaries having been settled, Anne made her first official appearance as queen on 13 April, Easter Sunday. She was 'loaded with diamonds and other precious stones, and dressed in a gorgeous suit of tissue' with a long train that was carried by the Duke of Norfolk's daughter, Mary Howard, soon to be married to Henry Fitzroy, the king's illegitimate son. 'She has now changed her title of marchioness for that of queen, and preachers specially name her so in their church prayers,' Chapuys wrote gloomily. 'At which all people here are perfectly astonished, for the whole thing seems a dream, and even those who support her party do not know whether to laugh or cry at it.'[10]

While proceedings in Rome went on at their stately pace, Cranmer held a court at Dunstable to pass upon the validity of Henry's marriage to Katherine. As Katherine did not recognise the authority of the court and thus refused to appear, she was declared contumacious, and the case moved only more expeditiously to its foregone conclusion. Cranmer then validated Henry's second marriage. All that remained was to put a crown on Anne's head.

Anne was crowned on 1 June 1533. Mary was certainly not present at the coronation ceremonies, and neither was Margaret. Given Margaret's presence at the coronations of Elizabeth of York and Katherine of Aragon, the thought of Anne receiving the crown must have been particularly galling to her. Another prominent absentee was Sir Thomas More. When Cuthbert Tunstall, Bishop of Durham, Stephen Gardiner, Bishop of Winchester, and John Clerk, Bishop of Bath and Wales, sent the ex-chancellor twenty pounds

to buy a gown for the festivities, More kept the twenty pounds –
he explained that he was not wealthy and was in need of a new
gown – but stayed home on coronation day. As More's son-in-law
Thomas Roper wrote, More told the bishops that their request

> did put me in remembrance of an emperor that had ordained
> a law that whosoever committed a certain offense (which
> I now remember not) except it were a virgin, should suffer
> the pains of death, such a reverence had he for virginity. Now
> so it happened that the first committer of that offense was
> indeed a virgin, whereof the Emperor hearing was in no small
> perplexity, as he that by some example fain would have had
> that law to have been put in execution. Whereupon when his
> Council had sat long, solemnly debating this case, suddenly
> arose there up one of his Council, a good plain man, among
> them, and said, 'Why make you so much ado, my lords,
> about so small a matter? Let her first be deflowered, and then
> after may she be devoured.' And so though your lordships
> have in the matter of the matrimony hitherto kept yourselves
> pure virgins, yet take good heed, my lords, that you keep
> your virginity still. For some there be that by procuring your
> lordships first at the coronation to be present, and next to
> preach for the setting forth of it, and finally to write books
> to all the world in defence thereof, are desirous to deflower
> you; and when they have deflowered you, then will they not
> fail soon after to devour you. Now my lords, it lieth not in
> my power but that they may devour me; but God being my
> good lord, I will provide that they shall never deflower me.[11]

If Margaret's family shared More's reservations, they kept this
to themselves. Francis, Lord Hastings, who was Lord Montagu's
son-in-law, was among those made Knights of the Bath on 30 May
during the traditional lead-up to the coronation, and Geoffrey Pole
was a server at the coronation banquet. Lord Montagu is named in
one record as the queen's carver, although it appears that he was

replaced by the Earl of Essex.[12] Nonetheless, both Lord Montagu and Geoffrey, along with Hastings, dined with Mary four days after the coronation.[13]

Mary and her household did not have to wait long to feel the impact of the king's new marriage. As Anne confidently awaited the birth of her child, Henry's minister Thomas Cromwell ordered Mary's hapless chamberlain, Lord Hussey, to turn Mary's jewels over to Mistress Frances Elmer. Margaret, as Hussey reported to Cromwell on 21 August 1533, was not inclined to be cooperative:

> I thank you for your kindness; advertising you that on the King's command and your letter that Mrs. Franc[e]s Elmer should have the custody of the Princess's jewels, I spake with my lady governess to have an inventory made, and the jewels delivered as the King desired. On calling for an inventory, to charge her that had the custody of them and her executors, none could be found. The most that I could get my said Lady to do was to bring forth the jewels and set my hand to the inventory she had made. But she will not deliver the jewels to Mrs. Franc[e]s unless you obtain the King's letters to her in that behalf. Would to God that the King and you did know what I have had to do here of late.[14]

Soon after this, a second request came, this time for plate. Margaret informed Lord Hussey that the plate was in use at all seasons and could not be spared unless more was purchased, though she did allow that she would surrender the plate if the king insisted upon it.[15]

Margaret no doubt suspected that the interest in Mary's jewels and plate was a portent, and she was quite right. On 7 September 1533, Anne gave birth to a daughter, Elizabeth. The infant's arrival meant that the status of her older half-sister had to be addressed – and addressed it would be, most ruthlessly. Katherine of Aragon anticipated the treatment that would be meted out to her daughter when, in a letter that is undated but probably refers to this time period, she advised Mary, 'Almighty God will prove you, and I am very glad of it, for I trust He doth handle you with a good love … take heed of His commandments, and keep them as near as He will give you grace to do, for then are you sure armed.' Guessing that this was a tense time for Mary's governess as well, Katherine concluded her letter, 'I pray you recommend me unto my good lady of Salisbury, and pray her to have a good heart, for we never come to the kingdom of Heaven but by troubles.'[16] These troubles came in December, when Thomas Howard, Duke of Norfolk, was sent to Mary's residence of Beaulieu to inform the young woman that she would have to break up her household – which in October 1533 contained 162 people, including the Countess of Salisbury and her own entourage of one chaplain, one gentleman, two gentlewomen, one chamberer, two yeomen and two grooms – and join the entourage of her baby sister, who had been taken from London to the healthier climes of Hatfield.[17] As Eustace Chapuys reported:

The duke of Norfolk went himself to the Princess, and signified her father's pleasure that she should attend Court, and enter the service of his other bastard daughter [Elizabeth], whom the Duke deliberately, and in her presence, called princess of Wales. Upon which princess Mary replied: 'That is a title which belongs to me by right, and to no one else;' after which she addressed to him many gracious, honest, and very wise remonstrances, all tending to show that the proposals the Duke had brought from the King were both strange and unfitting. Which argument on the part of the Princess the Duke was unable to combat, so much so that he said to her that he had not gone thither to dispute, but to see the King's wishes accomplished, and his commands executed, namely, that she should be removed to the house taken for the bastard. Upon which the Princess, seeing that all her arguments and excuses would be of no avail, asked for half an hour's time to retire to her private chamber; where she remained, as I am given to understand, all the while, or nearly so, occupied in drawing out the protest whereof I once gave her the words. Thus, should she in any way be compelled by force or persuaded by deceit to renounce her rights, marry against her will, or enter a cloister, no prejudice should result to her hereafter.

When she came out of her room the Princess said to the Duke: 'Since such is my father's wish, it is not for me to disobey his injunctions; but I beg you to intercede with him that the services of many well deserving and trusty officers of my household may be rewarded, and one year's wages at least given to them.' After this she asked the Duke how many of her own servants she would be allowed to retain and take with her. The answer was that as she would find plenty of servants to attend on her where she was going, no great train of followers was needed. Accordingly the Princess set out on her journey, accompanied only by very few of her household. Her governess, daughter of the late duke of Clarence, and the King's near relative—a very honourable and virtuous lady, if there be one in England—offered, I hear, to serve the Princess at her own cost, with a good and honourable train of servants, but her offers were not accepted; nor will they ever be, for were the said lady to remain by the Princess they would no longer be able to execute their bad designs, which are evidently either to cause her to die of grief or in some other way, or else to compel her to renounce her rights, marry some low fellow, or let her fall a prey to lust, so that they may have a pretext and excuse for disinheriting her, and submitting her to all manner of bad treatment.[18]

After years of devoted service to Mary, Margaret had been summarily dismissed.

This was not Margaret's only trouble during the year of 1533. Elizabeth Barton, known as the 'Holy Maid of Kent', had acquired a reputation as a visionary and had attracted a following of those low and high as a result.[19] Even the king had given her audiences. Barton disapproved of Henry's marital shenanigans, however, and despite Thomas More's sensible advice to avoid speaking of 'any such manner things as pertain to princes' affairs, or the state of the realm', predicted that 'in case his highness proceeded to the accomplishment of the said divorce and married another, that then his majesty should not be king of this realm by the space of one month after'. For good measure, Barton added, Mary 'should prosper and reign in this kingdom and have many friends to sustain and maintain her'. Prophesies of this nature did not sit well with the king, and in late September, Barton was arrested. Upon questioning, she revealed that she had mentioned her prophesies about the king to a number of high-ranking people. Her associate Hugh Rich, a Friar Observant, in turn acknowledged showing Barton's revelations to Mary, Margaret, Lord and Lady Hussey, the Marchioness of Exeter, the Bishop of Exeter, Lady Derby and Sir Thomas More, to mention only the most eminent names on the list. Thomas Cromwell's memoranda suggests that Margaret may have been questioned about her link with Barton, but unlike the Marchioness of Exeter, who felt it necessary to write a couple of grovelling letters explaining away her contact with Barton as the weakness of 'a woman, whose fragility and brittleness is easily seduced and brought to abusion and light belief', Margaret's involvement does not seem to have run deep enough to bring her into trouble. Nonetheless, it might well have been remembered by the king when Margaret made her request to continue serving Mary at her own expense. Certainly, Henry's respect for Margaret diminished over time, for in February 1535, when Chapuys proposed that the ailing Mary be returned to the care of 'her old gouvernante, the countess of Salisbury, whom she regarded as her second mother', the king replied that the Countess was 'a fool, of no experience, and that if his daughter had been under her care during this illness she would have died, for she would not have known what to do'.[20] Whether this was because of the Barton episode or because Henry's struggles with Mary and Katherine of Aragon had poisoned his opinion of everyone associated with them, we cannot know.

Whether it was from the weight of the events of 1533 or a completely unrelated cause, Margaret fell ill in 1534. On 12 February, her son Lord Montagu wrote to Lady Lisle, whose husband, Arthur Plantagenet, Lord Lisle, was the illegitimate son of Edward IV and thus was yet another cousin of Margaret's. After thanking Lady Lisle for some herring, he reported, 'My lady my mother lies at Bisham, to whom I made your ladyship's recommendations. I assure you she is very weak, but it was to her great comfort to hear of my lord and your ladyship.'[21] By 6 March, however, Margaret was feeling well enough to write to Lord Lisle, who was serving as Deputy of Calais, on behalf of Richard Baker, who had previously served in Mary's household.

> Mine own good Cousin, In my most hearty manner I recommend me unto you, and to my Lady, your wife, being glad to hear of your good health: praying you that where my friend Richard Baker is by your favour appointed to the King's service in Calais, it [may] please you to be good lord unto him, and the rather for my sake, in all such things as ye may do him favour therein. For I do not but that ye shall find him an honest man, and meet to do the King service. And thus I pray Jesu preserve you in good health, and prosperous, to his pleasure.
> At Bisham, the vith day of March
> by your loving cousin
> Margaret Salysbery[22]

Another correspondent who took up Baker's cause was Sir Richard Tuke, who told Lord Lisle that Baker's wife, Alice, had been Margaret's woman at an earlier period and was 'a great treasure' for her good character and honesty.[23]

During this same period, Bishop Fisher and Thomas More were accused of misprision of treason arising out of their connection with Elizabeth Barton. Fisher was fined, but More talked his way out of trouble – for the time being. In March 1534, Parliament passed the Act of Succession, which disinherited Mary and ensured that the crown would pass to the still hoped-for son of Anne Boleyn, or, if such a boy failed to materialise, to Henry's daughter

Elizabeth. All of the king's subjects were required to take an oath upholding the act, the penalty for not doing so being misprision of high treason.[24]

Henry Pole, present at the 1534 parliament, likely took the oath there; presumably the rest of Margaret's family in England did as well.[25] Others, however, defied the king. Fisher (who despite his attainder had not been imprisoned) and More each refused to take the oath, the latter protesting that he was willing to swear to the succession but not to take the oath. This fine point was wasted upon the commissions appointed to carry out the king's orders, and More, like Fisher, thus earned a one-way trip to the Tower on 17 April. Three days later, the oath was given to the general populace of London, whose cooperation, as Richard Rex has pointed out, was likely encouraged by the dreadful sight of Elizabeth Barton's execution: 'This day the Nun of Kent, with ii Friars Observants, ii monks, and one secular priest, were drawn from the Tower to Tyburn, and there hanged and headed. God, if it be his pleasure, have mercy on their souls,' John Hussee wrote to Lord Lisle.[26]

In November 1534, Parliament followed up the Act of Succession with the Act of Supremacy, placing Henry at the head of the Church of England. This legislation was complemented by the Treason Act, which, as John Bellamy has explained, was focused on treasonous language. Wishing or attempting bodily harm to the king, his queen or the royal heir, or trying to deprive the king of his title by malicious deeds, writings and spoken words, or pronouncing the king a heretic, schismatic, tyrant, infidel or usurper was now deemed treason. All of these things had to be done 'maliciously', a word which as Bellamy points out was likely mere verbiage but nonetheless would provide a point of argument for some of those who would soon feel the statute's bite.[27]

As Fisher and More bided their time in the Tower, their resolve unshaken, Henry began to carry out his new laws. Those who had the dubious honour of being prosecuted first were John Houghton, the prior of the Charterhouse of London, Robert Lawrence, prior of the Charterhouse of Beauvale, Augustine Webster, prior of the Charterhouse of Axholme, Richard Reynolds, a monk from Syon, and John Hale, the parson of Isleworth, who like More and Fisher had declined to take the oath. The government had not wished to make martyrs out of them, but had made repeated attempts to win them over.[28] Persuasion proving futile, the men headed for trial, and eventual martyrdom, in April 1535. Lord Montagu was one of those ordered to serve on the commission of oyer and terminer; among the nobles who served with him were the queen's father and her brother.[29] The men having been convicted of high treason, on 4 May they died horrifically at Tyburn:

> [The five men] were drawn from the Tower of London to the place of execution (about a French league distant) and without respect for their Order hanged with great ropes. While they were still alive the hangman cut out their hearts and bowels and burned them. Then they were beheaded and quartered, and the parts placed in public places on long spears. And it is believed that one saw the other's execution fully carried out before he died,—a pitiful and strange spectacle, for it is long since persons have been known to die with greater constancy. No change was noticed in their colour or tone of speech, and while the execution was going on they preached and exhorted the bystanders with the greatest boldness to do well and obey the King in everything that was not against the honor of God and the Church.[30]

Chapuys claimed in disgust, 'the dukes of Richmond and Norfolk, the earl of Wiltshire (Thomas), his son (George), and several other lords and gentlemen courtiers, were present at the execution, openly and quite close to the victims. It is even reported that the King himself showed a desire to witness the butchery; which is likely enough, considering that nearly all his courtiers, even his own privy and principal chamberlain, Master No[r]ris, with 40 horsemen [of the King's body-guard], attended'.[31]

The day of 19 June 1535 saw the executions by hanging and quartering at Tyburn of three more Carthusians, Sebastian Newdigate, William Exmew and Humphrey Middlemore. Ultimately, eighteen Carthusians would be martyred, most dying through neglect in prison.[32]

Three days later, Bishop Fisher was beheaded at Tower Hill, following a trial by a commission of oyer and terminer on 17 June.[33] His indictment states that he had denied the royal supremacy on 7 May. The Pope may well have unwittingly hastened his end by making him a cardinal on 20 May, an attempt at safeguarding his life which served only to infuriate the king. According to William Rastell, Fisher had been entrapped by Richard Rich, the king's solicitor general, into giving his opinion under the guise that he would suffer no penalty if he gave his frank opinion of the royal supremacy; having given it, he found it being used against him at trial, leaving him to argue unsuccessfully that he had not spoken 'maliciously', in the words of the Treason Act.

Led to the execution spot on a mule, Fisher had to wait for an hour, according to the Bishop of Faenza, before the scaffold was made ready for its task. Having finally reached his destination, Fisher duly observed execution tradition, 'telling [the observers] to be loving and obedient to their King, who was good by nature, but had been deceived in this matter'. His end was a particularly poignant one, for he owed his career to the patronage of Henry's grandmother Margaret Beaufort, Countess of Richmond. One suspects that the countess, a veteran of the internecine strife between Lancaster and York in the fifteenth century, would nonetheless have been horrified at Fisher's brutal end. She would likely have also been angered that Fisher's fine library, which the bishop had earmarked for St John's College, Cambridge, founded by the Countess of Richmond, never made it to its intended destination.

Sad as Fisher's end was, he was not entirely an abject innocent; it appears that he had been intriguing against the king (or at the very least engaging in some dangerous musing) back in the autumn of 1533 – and including Margaret and her son Reginald Pole in his calculations.[34] Chapuys, writing in support of Katherine of Aragon and Mary, informed Emperor Charles:

That excellent and holy man, the bishop of Rochester, told me some time ago, the Pope's weapons become very malleable when directed against the obdurate and pertinacious, and, therefore, it is incumbent upon Your Majesty to interfere in this affair, and undertake a work which must be as pleasing in the eyes of God as war upon the Turk. Indeed, should there be a question of coming to a rupture [with England] it would not be amiss for Your Majesty to try by all possible means to have at your court, or elsewhere under your power, the son of the Princess' governess [Margaret], the daughter of the duke of Clarence [George], upon whom, in the opinion of many people here, the succession to the Crown would by right devolve. Owing to the said duke's great and singular virtues, her son [Reginald Pole] is now studying at the Paduan University, to which circumstance may be added that being closely related to this king, both on the father's and mother's side, he and his brothers might easily lay claim to the succession to the kingdom. For this reason the Queen wishes for a marriage in that quarter as much, or perhaps more than in any other, and the Princess herself; far from refusing it, would, I have no doubt, gladly give her consent. The youth and his brothers have many relatives and allies [among the nobility] besides a very numerous party whose affections Your Majesty might by such means easily gain, and thus secure those of the rest of this nation.[35]

It would not be the last time Reginald's name was linked to treason.

Fisher's parboiled head – by some accounts said to be looking 'every day fresher and fresher'[36] – was still sitting on its perch on London Bridge, next to the Carthusian monks, when the next casualty of that summer came to the scaffold: Sir Thomas More.

More's trial took place on 1 July. Among the judges were Thomas, Duke of Norfolk (uncle to Anne Boleyn), Charles, Duke of Suffolk (married to the king's sister Mary), Thomas Boleyn, Earl of Wiltshire (the queen's father), George Boleyn, Lord Rochford (the queen's brother), Thomas Audley, Lord Chancellor, and Thomas Cromwell.[37] Henry Pole, Lord Montagu, was also appointed to the commission of oyer and terminer to try More, but Duncan Derrett notes that he did not take his place there.[38] This may have been due to indisposition (as we shall see shortly, he was reported dangerously ill a few days later), but it may have also been that he found an excuse to avoid sitting in judgment of a man with whom his family had been on excellent terms. Years before, the apparently ailing More had written to John Clement and Reginald Pole, then at Oxford, to thank them for their solicitude for their health, and had added, 'I thank you, my dear Pole, doubly for deigning to procure for me the advice of so skilful a physician, and no less for obtaining from your mother – noblest and best of women, and fully worthy of such a son, the remedy prescribed and for getting it made up.' More had also proudly informed his scholarly daughter, Margaret Roper, that 'a young man of the noblest rank and of the widest attainments in literature ... as conspicuous for his piety as he is for his learning' had been dumbfounded to realise that his daughter was the author of a letter More had shown him; the man whose opinion pleased More so much was likely Reginald Pole.[39]

The star witness was Solicitor General Richard Rich, who had turned up at More's prison cell in June to seize his books and writing materials and, it appears, to entrap him into treason. Rich claimed that as his companions busied themselves with removing More's cherished books, he entered into a discussion with More, who stated that Parliament had no authority to make the king the supreme head of the church. Too weak to stand for his trial, More nonetheless mounted a vigorous defence, accusing Rich of perjury and attacking his character. Telling Rich that he was 'sorrier for your perjury than for my own peril', he reminded his accuser that they lived in the same parish, where 'you were esteemed to be very light of tongue, a great dicer, and of no commendable fame. And so in your house at the Temple, where has been your chief bringing up, were you likewise accounted.' Turning to his judges, More asked, 'Can it therefore seem likely to your honourable lordships that I would, in so weighty a cause, so unadvisedly overshoot myself as to trust Master Rich, a man by me always reputed for one of very little truth ... that I would utter to him the secrets of my conscience touching the king's supremacy?' More's defence rattled Rich sufficiently for him to call his companions at the interview, Sir Richard Southwell and Master Thomas Palmer, to corroborate his story, but to no avail. Both men claimed, rather improbably, to have been so absorbed in seizing the bibliophilic More's library that they had paid no heed to the conversation between him and Rich.

Despite this poor evidentiary showing, More was promptly found guilty. But More was not yet done. As Audley, the chancellor, prepared to pass the grim sentence upon him, the prisoner, himself a lawyer and former chancellor, interrupted to remind him that it was the custom to ask the prisoner why judgment should not be given against him, then to protest against his indictment as 'grounded upon an Act of Parliament directly repugnant to the laws of God and His Holy Church'. Continuing in this vein, More managed to thoroughly discomfit his judges, but the victory was fleeting, ending as soon as Audley resumed his task of pronouncing the sentence. More's execution was scheduled for 6 July, the same day the court was departing on a progress.

Not wanting his hair shirt exposed to public view as he was stripped to his undergarments during his execution, More sent it, along with an affectionate letter, to his daughter on 5 July. The next morning, Sir Thomas Pope came from the king and his council to announce, as More had already surmised, that he would die that day. Pope brought the order that More refrain from 'using many words' on the scaffold, but also assured him that the king would allow his family to attend his burial. With Pope's departure, More dressed in his best clothing for his execution, only to be dissuaded by the Lieutenant of the Tower, William Kingston (who in less than a year would be presiding over an even more high-profile execution), that the executioner, who would be getting More's clothing as a perquisite of the job, was a 'worthless fellow' who would make ill use of it. More settled for sending the executioner a gold coin known as an angel and changing into a less costly garment.

> And so was he brought by Mr. Lieutenant out of the Tower, and from thence led towards the place of execution, where going up the scaffold, which was so weak that it was ready to fall, he said to Mr. Lieutenant, 'I pray you, I pray you, Mr. Lieutenant, see me safe up, and for my coming down let me shift for myself.' Then desired he all the people thereabouts to pray for him, and to bear witness with him, that he should then suffer death in and for the faith of the holy Catholic Church, which done he kneeled down, and after his prayers said, he turned to the executioner, and with a cheerful countenance spake unto him. 'Pluck up thy spirits, man, and be not afraid to do thine office, my neck is very short. Take heed therefore thou shoot not awry for saving thine honesty.' So passed Sir Thomas More out of this world to God.[40]

Reginald Pole would later write to the king, of the deaths of More and the rest, 'From the time that I heard of the slaughter of those men, I do not deny that I lay senseless and unable to speak for almost a month, so stunned was I by the novelty and wonder of such unheard-of cruelty.'[41]

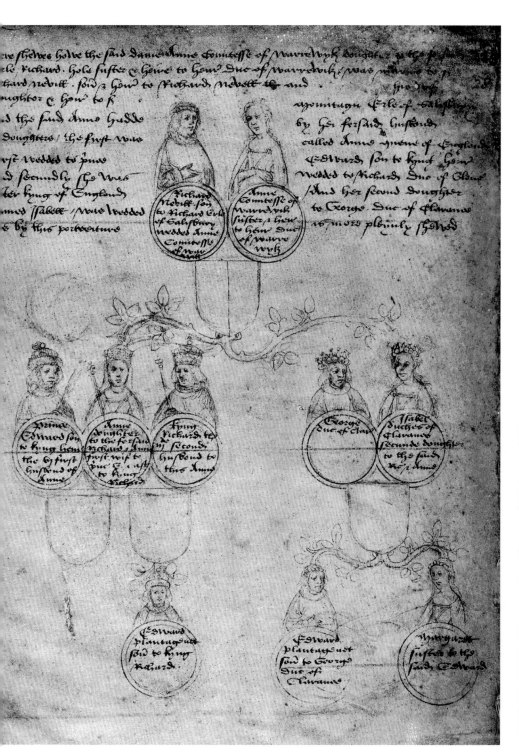

1. Genealogical illustration from the Beauchamp Pageant showing the descendants of Richard Neville, Earl of Warwick, and his countess, Anne Beauchamp (top). Margaret , her parents, and her brother are on the right; Anne Neville, her husbands (Edward of Lancaster and Richard III), and her son by Richard III are on the left.

2. Drawing of Margaret and her brother by unknown artist based on illustration in the Rous Roll, along with Richard III, his queen, and their son.

3. Remains of Farleigh Hungerford Castle, birthplace of Margaret.

4. Interior of Tewkesbury Abbey, resting place of Margaret's parents, the Duke and Duchess of Clarence.

5. Painting thought to be of Margaret, Countess of Salisbury. Note the barrel on her wrist.

CARDENALL POOLL

6. Reginald Pole.

7. Surviving tower of Warblington Castle, built to Margaret's specifications.

THE COUNTESS OF SALISBURY'S CHAPEL, PRIORY CHURCH, CHRISTCHUCH, HANTS

8. Margaret's chapel, Priory Church, Christchurch, Hampshire.

Above: 9. Three Roman Catholic martyrs executed on the orders of Henry VIII. Bishop Fisher in 1535, Thomas More 1535, and the Countess of Salisbury in 1541. Engraving of 1587.

Right: 10. Church of St Mary, Stoughton, West Sussex. Burial place of Geoffrey Pole and his wife, Constance.

Below right: 11. Effigies of Catherine Pole, Countess of Huntingdon, and her husband Francis Hastings, Earl of Huntingdon, at St Helen's Church, Ashby-de-la-Zouch. Catherine, Henry Pole's daughter, began corresponding with her uncle Reginald Pole after Mary came to the throne.

Above: 12. Henry Hastings, Earl of Huntingdon, great-grandson of Margaret through her son Henry, Lord Montagu.

Left: 13. George, Duke of Clarence, from the Rous Roll.

14. Elizabeth Woodville from the Martyrdom Chapel at Canterbury Cathedral.

EDWARDVS. IIII

15. Edward IV, who ordered the execution of Margaret's father, George, Duke of Clarence.

Above: 16. Richard III.

Left: 17. Henry VII. The Lancastrian king ordered the execution of Margaret's younger brother Edward, Earl of Warwick.

Above left: 18. Elizabeth of York.

Above right: 19. Henry VIII. The king ordered Margaret's botched execution.

20. Katherine of Aragon, close friend to Margaret.

ANNA BOLLINA VXOR HEN VIII.

21. Anne Boleyn.

22. Princess Mary, later to become Queen Mary I. Margaret was governess to the young Mary.

Right: 23. Thomas More.

Below: 24. Bishop Fisher.

Left: 25. The Tower of London.

Below: 26. Site of the execution of Margaret Pole.

8

HONOUR AND CONSCIENCE

Margaret stayed well out of the public eye during the bloody year of 1535. Only in one controversy did she involve herself: the appointment of William Barlow to the priory of Bisham. Sir Nicholas Carew, writing to Thomas Cromwell on 27 April, noted dryly that the current prior, with the support of Margaret and others, refused to resign, although Margaret and the rest had thought the current prior unsuited for the position before Cromwell put forth the reform-minded Barlow as a candidate. The dispute was heated enough for Carew to grumble, 'I would have had spent a hundred pounds I had never spoken in it for somewhat it toucheth my poor honesty', but Barlow's supporters carried the day. Barlow went on to become Bishop of Chichester during Elizabeth's reign.[1]

Around the time of More's execution, Lord Montagu fell ill – so much so that John Hussee reported to Lord Lisle on 7 July 1535, 'The saying is that my Lord Montague is sore sick or dead.' His news was echoed by another correspondent, Leonard Smyth, who informed Lady Lisle that Lord Montagu was 'sore sick and like to die'. By 12 July, however, Hussee was able to tell Lady Lisle that Lord Montagu was expected to recover, and on 20 July he was walking about. The next day, Lord Montagu was so improved that Hussee wrote to Lady Lisle, 'My Lord Montague is recovered and walking, thanked be God', before rushing to the next subject, a monkey that Lady Lisle had proposed to send to Anne Boleyn, who, however, could 'scant abide the sight of them'.[2] The time was coming, however, when no one would care what Anne thought.

After Margaret's dismissal from Mary's household in October 1533, Mary had most unwillingly joined the household of her baby sister, Elizabeth, at Hatfield, having first written a vehement protest, under the guidance of Eustace Chapuys:

> My lords, as touching my removing to Hatfield, I will obey his Grace, as my duty is, or to any other place that his Grace will appoint me. But I protest before you and all other that be here present, that my conscience will in no wise suffer me to take any other than my self for the king's lawful daughter, born in true matrimony or princess, and that I will never willingly and wittingly say or do, whereby any person might take occasion to think that I agree to the contrary, not of any ambition or proud mind, as God is my judge: but that if I should say or do otherwise, I should in my conscience slander the deed of our mother holy church and the Pope, who is the judge in this matter, & none other: and also dishonor the king my Father, the Queen my Mother, and falsely confess myself a Bastard, which God defend that I should do, seeing the Pope hath not so declared it by his sentence definitive, for to his iudgement I submit me.[3]

Mary had kept up this defiant stance, much to the utter exasperation of everyone around her and to the surprise of King Henry and Queen Anne. Men like Fisher and More who refused to bow to the king's will could be imprisoned and executed, but Henry could do little more than engage in a war of attrition against Mary. For her part, Anne Boleyn vacillated between complaining that the king did not keep his stubborn daughter 'close enough' (i.e. isolated) and making overtures of peace, as when she promised Mary while on a visit to Elizabeth that if she accepted her as queen, she would see to it that Mary was treated as well or better than ever. Unmoved, Mary coolly replied that she knew no queen in England except for her mother, but would be much obliged if Madame Boleyn assisted her. Small wonder that Anne stormed away from the encounter vowing to 'bring down the pride of this unbridled Spanish blood'.[4]

With the passage of the Act of Succession in March 1534, Katherine and Mary's positions became more desperate. Katherine, who naturally refused to take the required oath under the Act, went so far as to hint that the Emperor Charles should launch an invasion of England; as Chapuys reported in May, 'she now perceives that it is absolutely necessary to apply stronger remedies to the evil. What these are to be, she durst not point out – firstly, because she is afraid of her letters being intercepted; and secondly, lest she should contradict in the least what she has said and written on former occasions. She is also aware that Your Majesty knows best what sort of remedy matters in this country require. Whatever that remedy may be, it must be applied shortly.'[5] Meanwhile, Henry was once again in pleading mode with his daughter: 'During the last few days the King, perceiving that neither by force nor menaces could he get his way with the said Princess, or for some other reasons, has shown her more honour than usual, and used more gracious words, begging that she would lay aside her obstinacy and he would promise her before Michaelmas to make such a bargain with her that she should enjoy a royal title and dignity; to which, among 1,000 other wise answers, she replied that God had not so blinded her as to confess for any kingdom on earth that the King her father and the Queen her mother had so long lived in adultery, nor would she contravene the ordinance of the Church and make herself a bastard. She believes firmly that this dissimulation the King uses is only the more easily to attain his end and cover poison, but she says she cares little, having full confidence in God that she will go straight to Paradise and be quit of the tribulations of this world, and her only grief is about the troubles of the Queen her mother.'[6]

In February 1535, it appeared that Mary might get her wish, for she fell seriously ill. Said to be 'as much grieved at her sickness as any father could be for his daughter', Henry (ironically using Thomas Boleyn, the best French speaker at court, as an intermediary) summoned Chapuys and arranged for his own physician and one or two of Chapuys' own selection to visit the ailing princess. Such a crisis might have brought out the best in some families, but this royal family was having none of it. Katherine, insinuating that Mary (who was quickly found to be suffering from 'only her usual illness', a female complaint) might have been poisoned, asked to nurse her personally; Henry refused and railed against Mary's stubbornness and disobedience. It was at this time that Chapuys, as ever steering between these two immovable objects, reported that Henry had refused his offer to send Margaret to nurse Mary on the ground that she was 'a fool, of no experience, and that if his daughter had been under her care during this illness she would have died, for she would not have known what to do, whereas her present governess is an expert lady even in such female complaints'. Chapuys passed along some gossip to the Emperor: Thomas, Duke of Norfolk, had retreated from court in a huff, complaining to Lord Montagu that he was held in no esteem due to the malign influence of Anne Boleyn, and Henry's eye, which had strayed toward an unidentified young lady, had now strayed away from her in the direction of a cousin of Anne Boleyn.[7]

With the deaths of Fisher, More and the Carthusian monks, Katherine's and Mary's positions became considerably more perilous, and their actions increasingly reckless. Chapuys claimed that Anne Boleyn was 'incessantly crying after the King that he does not act with prudence in suffering the Queen and Princess to live, who deserved death more than those who have been executed, and that they were the cause of all'. In October 1535, Katherine wrote to the Pope, informing him that 'if a remedy be not applied shortly, there will be no end to ruined souls and martyred saints', and to the Emperor, praying him 'to him to urge the Pope to look to the remedy of her affairs'.[8] Mary wrote an even more incendiary letter, which if found would have confirmed all of Anne Boleyn's suspicions of her:

Although I am sure that, prompted by His innate virtue, goodness, and magnanimity, His Majesty has had due regard for the many and singular services which you, Chapuys, have, and are continually rendering him, yet I should feel it as one of the greatest mishaps of my sad fortune, were I not allowed time and opportunity to acknowledge those which for a considerable length of time you have rendered to the Queen, my mother, and to myself. Now more than ever those services on your part are urgently required, considering the miserable plight and wretched condition of affairs in this country, which is such that unless His Majesty, the Emperor, for the service of God, the welfare and repose of Christendom, as well as the honor of the King, my father, takes pity on these poor afflicted creatures, all and everything will go to total ruin, and be irretrievably lost. For the Emperor to apply a prompt remedy, as I hope and trust he will, it is necessary that he should be well and minutely informed of the state of affairs in this country. And although I suppose, nay believe as certain, that you have hitherto done good offices in that respect, yet, considering that His Majesty has for a long time back been occupied in that very glorious and no less holy and necessary undertaking of Tunis, and may not perhaps have acquired the information needful respecting the nature, weight, importance, and dangerous position of affairs in this country; as moreover it is not easy to convey by ciphered letters an exact and minute account of the whole, I would dare ask this favour of you, – that you dispatch forthwith one of your men, an able one and possessing such information, to the Emperor, and inform him of the whole, and beg him, in the name of the Queen, my mother, and mine, for the honour of God, and the considerations above mentioned, to take this matter in hand, and provide a remedy for the affairs of this country. The work itself will be highly acceptable in the eyes of God, and no less glory will be gained by it than by the conquest of Tunis, or even that of Africa; begging you in the meantime not to forget to solicit permission for me to live with my mother, or else obtain leave for her to come, or send her people to visit me. I should very much wish to write to His Majesty in my own hand, but not knowing how to thank him in due measure for what he has already done for the Queen, my mother, or for myself, and, on the other hand, fearing lest those who are constantly watching me should get hold of the letter, I have hitherto been unable to accomplish my wish, though I find some consolation and comfort in the idea that you yourself will supply the want, and do and say in my name what is proper and fit.

To cap off her defiance, Mary signed her letter (written in French): 'Marye, princesse.'[9]

Gertrude Courtenay, Marchioness of Exeter, who had already been compromised in the Elizabeth Barton affair and who would soon find herself involved in far more dangerous matters, was keeping a close watch on affairs at court. In November 1535, Chapuys reported to the Emperor, 'The marchioness of Exeter has sent to inform me that the King has lately said to some of his most confidential councillors that he would no longer remain in the trouble, fear, and suspense he had so long endured on account of the Queen and Princess, and that they should see, at the coming parliament, to get him released therefrom, swearing most obstinately that he would wait no longer. The Marchioness declares this is as true as the Gospel, and begs me to inform your Majesty and pray you to have pity upon the ladies, and for the honour of God and the bond of kin to find a, remedy.'[10]

The remedy came soon enough, but through a higher power than either the Pope or the Emperor. In late December, Henry VIII's first queen fell ill at her residence of Kimbolton. On 7 January, she died. She had sent for Chapuys, who, having obtained the necessary royal permission, spent four days with her. On the fourth day, Katherine was so much improved and in such good spirits that Chapuys, not wanting to 'abuse the licence' he had been granted by the king, left for London, riding slowly in case he had to be summoned back to Kimbolton. No message came, and Chapuys returned to London only to be told by Cromwell that Katherine had died. 'The good Queen breathed her last at 2 o'clock in the afternoon,' Chapuys wrote.[11]

Margaret had known Katherine since the latter came to England as an adolescent to marry Prince Arthur, and her passing must have deeply affected the countess, as it did Chapuys, who could not 'find words strong enough to express his sorrow'. Not so the king and Anne Boleyn. Anne, according to the chronicler Hall, bedecked herself in yellow, while Chapuys reported that Henry exclaimed, 'Thank God, we are now free from any fear of war!' and donned his own yellow robes, save for a white feather in his cap, and showed off his little daughter Elizabeth: 'Then, after dinner, the King went to the hall, where the ladies were dancing, and there made great demonstration of joy, and at last went into his own apartments, took the little bastard, carried her in his arms, and began to show her first to one, then to another, and did the same on the following days. Since then his joy has somewhat subsided; he has no longer made such demonstrations, but to make up for it, as it were, has been tilting and running lances at [Greenwich].'[12]

Mary, according to Chapuys, bore her mother's death with 'great sense and incomparable virtue' and asked him for advice on what to do if demanded to take the oath of allegiance.[13] Anne, meanwhile, was inclined to be generous to the now motherless Mary, and for good reason: not only was she the undisputed queen, she was expecting a second child. Accordingly, she sent word to Mary through her aunt that should she 'consent to wa[i]ve her obstinacy, and be obedient, like a dutiful daughter, to her father's commands, she (the concubine) would at once become her warmest friend, and a second mother to her, and that, if she wished to go to Court, she should be exempted from being her train-bearer, and might walk by her side'.[14] Mary, however, was unmoved, informing Lady Shelton, who had the thankless task of relaying the messages between these two strong-willed women, that she would rather 'die a hundred times than change her opinion or do anything against her honour and conscience'.[15]

As preparations went forward for Katherine's funeral, the court continued to enjoy itself – until 24 January. On this day, Henry fell from his horse while jousting and remained insensible for two hours.

'[H]e might ask of fortune for what greater misfortune he is reserved,' Chapuys grumbled upon reporting the king's recovery.[16] He would soon have more satisfactory news – from his point of view – to report.

Katherine of Aragon was buried at Peterborough Abbey on 28 January. Nothing indicates that Margaret attended the funeral, where the chief mourner was Eleanor, King Henry's niece through his sister Mary.[17] On that day or perhaps 30 January, Anne Boleyn miscarried what was believed to have been a son.[18] Anne blamed the Duke of Norfolk for having frightened her with news of the king's fall, but Chapuys scoffed at this; Norfolk, he said, had broken the news to her carefully. Rather, he said, '[s]ome think it was owing to her own incapacity to bear children, others to a fear that the King would treat her like the late Queen, especially considering the treatment shown to a lady of the Court, named Mistress Semel, to whom, as many say, he has lately made great presents'.[19]

This report, which is dated 10 February, is the first mention of Jane Seymour, the daughter of Sir John Seymour of Wiltshire and his wife, Margery Wentworth. Described later by Chapuys as 'of middle stature and no great beauty, so fair that one would call her pale rather than otherwise', she had served Katherine as a lady-in-waiting before making the transfer to Anne's court.[20] When Henry had become interested in her is unknown; he had visited the Seymour family seat of Wolf Hall during the progress of the previous autumn, and there would have been opportunities for him to see her at court as well. How deeply interested Henry was at this point is also unknown, although Chapuys recorded in January that Henry, having become convinced he had been seduced into marriage by witchcraft, was considering taking a third wife. Chapuys himself regarded the story with considerable scepticism, and even if the story were true, which seems unlikely since Anne had not yet had her miscarriage at the time, nothing indicates that Henry had a particular candidate in mind.[21]

As the weeks passed, Henry's interest in the pale young lady from Wiltshire grew apace, 'to the intense rage of the concubine'.[22] A faction of disaffected courtiers began to collect around Jane.

Among them was Margaret's son Lord Montagu, who in late March dined with Chapuys, and 'after many complaints of the disorder of affairs here, told [him] that the Concubine and Cromwell were on bad terms, and that some new marriage for the King was spoken of'. This, Chapuys noted, agreed with the intelligence he had heard that Henry was seeking a French princess. In fact, Montagu and the rest appear to have had a candidate closer to home in mind, for as Chapuys composed his report on 1 April, the ever-meddling Marchioness of Exeter hurried to tell him that Henry had sent Jane Seymour

a purse full of sovereigns, and with it a letter, and that the young lady, after kissing the letter, returned it unopened to the messenger, and throwing herself on her knees before him, begged the said messenger that he would pray the King on her part to consider that she was a gentlewoman of good and honorable parents, without reproach, and that she had no greater riches in the world than her honor, which she would not injure for a thousand deaths, and that if he wished to make her some present in money she begged it might be when God enabled her to make some honorable match.

The said Marchioness has sent to me to say that by this the King's love and desire towards the said lady was wonderfully increased, and that he had said she had behaved most virtuously, and to show her that he only loved her honorably, he did not intend henceforth to speak with her except in presence of some of her kin; for which reason the King has caused Cromwell to remove from a chamber to which the King can go by certain galleries without being perceived, and has lodged there the eldest brother of the said lady with his wife, in order to bring thither the same young lady, who has been well taught for the most part by those intimate with the King, who hate the concubine, that she must by no means comply with the King's wishes except by way of marriage; in which she is quite firm. She is also advised to tell the King boldly how his marriage is detested by the people, and none consider it lawful; and on the occasion when she shall bring forward the subject, there ought to be present none but titled persons, who will say the same if the King put them upon their oath of fealty. And the said Marchioness would like that I or some one else, on the part of your Majesty, should assist in the matter; and certainly it appears to me that if it succeed, it will be a great thing both for the security of the Princess and to remedy the heresies here, of which the Concubine is the cause and principal nurse, and also to pluck the King from such an abominable and more than incestuous marriage. The Princess would be very happy, even if she were excluded from her inheritance by male issue. I will consult with them again today, and on learning her opinion will consider the expedient to be taken, so that if no good be done, I may at least not do any harm.[23]

By the end of April, Geoffrey Pole had joined Jane's promoters. It was then that Chapuys, noting that Sir Nicholas Carew had been made a knight of the Garter instead of George Boleyn, Viscount Rochford, who had expected the honour, wrote:

[Carew] continually counsels [Mistress Seymour] and other conspirators '*pour luy faire une venue,*' and only four days ago he and some persons of the chamber sent to tell the Princess to be of good cheer, for shortly the opposite party would put water in their wine, for the King was already as sick and tired of the concubine as could be; and the brother of lord Montague told me yesterday at dinner that the day before the bishop of London had been asked if the King could abandon the said concubine, and he would not give any opinion to anyone but the King himself, and before doing so he would like to know the King's own inclination, meaning to intimate that the King might leave the said concubine, but that, knowing his fickleness, he would not put himself in danger.[24]

Margaret must have surely supported her sons' actions, and probably even encouraged them, for the sake of her relationship with Katherine of Aragon and her daughter. Any role she played, however, was extremely discreet, as it has left no trace in the records.

On 30 April, the day after Chapuys wrote the report mentioned above, Mark Smeaton, a musician in the queen's household, was arrested and taken to Cromwell's house for questioning. The next day, the king and queen were attending the May Day jousts at Greenwich when the king suddenly rode off with a small entourage that included Sir Henry Norris, the chief gentleman of his Privy Chamber, bound for Whitehall. Less than twenty-four hours later, Anne Boleyn and her brother were arrested and taken to the Tower, where Smeaton and Norris were already lodged. Over the next few days, Sir William Brereton, Sir Francis Weston, Sir Thomas Wyatt and Sir Richard Page joined them. Soon, all but Wyatt and Page would be on trial for their lives, the men charged with adultery with the queen – to which Smeaton had confessed.

Entire books can be, and have been, written about the events that brought a queen to the Tower, then to the scaffold.[25] While most historians believe that Anne and her accused lovers were innocent of the charges against them, the matter of whether the charges were brought in good faith – and if not, who was behind their fabrication – remains hotly disputed, and will likely always be unless additional documents surface. Some believe that the charges against the queen and her supposed lovers were a cynical ploy by the king to rid himself of a woman who had failed to bear him sons and who had lost his affection; to others, Thomas Cromwell, finding the queen a hindrance to his own schemes, is the villain of the piece. It may well be, however, that those who brought the charges believed at least partly in their truth and that the tragedy had rather haphazard origins: a quarrel between courtier siblings in which the brother questioned the sister's morals and the sister angrily rejoined that she was no worse than the queen herself, which sparked an investigation and the interrogation of Mark Smeaton. In turn, for reasons of his own – perhaps an unrequited obsession with the queen and a determination that if he could not have her, he would destroy himself, her and those whom he perceived as his more successful rivals – he confessed, and implicated others. Making matters worse, a few defendants had made highly indiscreet remarks, which made the charges, whatever their motivation and validity, more plausible. Some of the most compromising evidence came from the queen herself, who reported Smeaton's mooning after her, a conversation with Weston in which Weston professed to love Anne more than his wife, and Anne's remark to Norris that he was looking for 'dead men's shoes, for if ought came to the king but good you would like to have me'. (Norris, at least, understood the seriousness of discussing the king's death, even in courtly banter, and promptly declared that 'if he should have any such thought he would his head were off'.)

Weston, Norris, Brereton and Smeaton were tried at Westminster on 12 May; all pleaded not guilty except for Smeaton, who never recanted his confession. They were charged with adultery and with having 'conspired the death and destruction of the King, the queen often saying she would marry one of them as soon as the King died, and affirming that she would never love the king in her heart'.[26] In accordance with the law of the time, their guilt was presumed and the burden rested on them to prove their innocence. Having failed at this daunting task, all four were found guilty and sentenced to death – even Brereton, against whom no evidence survives.

Two days later, it was the turn of the queen and her brother, who were tried within the Tower in front of an audience that according to Chapuys numbered over 2,000. Henry, Lord Montagu, was one of the twenty-six peers appointed to try the two.[27] The queen was the first to be judged. In keeping with the standard practice of the time, at which live testimony was unusual, no witnesses were presented.[28] Instead, Sir Christopher Hales, the chief prosecutor, offered a narrative summary of the evidence, a highlight of which was that of Lady Wingfield, a former lady of the queen's who had made a sworn statement before her death. Sir John Spelman, who recorded an account of the trial, wrote that 'all the evidence was of bawdery and lechery, so that there was no such whore of the realm'.[29] Chapuys reported,

What she was principally charged with was having cohabited with her brother and other accomplices; that there was a promise between her and Norris to marry after the King's death, which it thus appeared they hoped for; and that she had received and given to Norris certain medals, which might be interpreted to mean that she had poisoned the late Queen and intrigued to do the same to the Princess. These things she totally denied, and gave to each a plausible answer. Yet she confessed she had given money to [Weston], as she had often done to other young gentlemen. She was also charged, and her brother likewise, with having laughed at the King and his dress, and that she showed in various ways she did not love the King but was tired of him.[30]

After Anne responded to the charges against her, Lord Montagu and his fellow peers returned a unanimous verdict of guilty, and Thomas Howard, Duke of Norfolk – presiding over his niece's trial – sentenced the queen to be burned or beheaded, the mode of execution being left to the king. Anne then responded:

My lords, I will not say that your sentence is unjust; nor presume that my opinion ought to be preferred to the judgment of you all. I believe you have reasons, and occasions and suspicions of jealously, upon which you have condemned me, but they must be other, than those that have been produced here in court, for I am entirely innocent of all these accusations; so that I cannot ask pardon of God for them. I have always been a faithful and loyal wife to the king. I have not, perhaps, at all times showed him that humility and reverence, that his goodness to me, and the honour to which he raised me, did deserve. I confess, I have had fancies and suspicions of him, which I had not strength nor discretion enough to manage; but God knows, and is my witness, that I never failed otherwise towards him; and I shall never confess any other, at the hour of my death. Do not think that I say this, on design to prolong my life: God has taught me to know how to die; and he will fortify my faith … As for my brother, and those others, who are unjustly condemned, I would willingly suffer many deaths, to deliver them, but since I see it so pleases the king, I must willingly bear with their death, and shall accompany them in death, with this assurance, that I shall lead an endless life with them in peace.[31]

Anne then left the courtroom, her dignified behaviour on the stand having left the spectators, if not the peers who judged her, with the belief that she was innocent.[32] George Boleyn, Viscount Rochford, then took the stand to face the particularly salacious charges against him, such as the accusation that the queen had 'procured and incited her own natural brother, Geo. Boleyn, lord Rochford, gentleman of the Privy Chamber, to violate her, alluring him with her tongue in the said George's mouth, and the said George's tongue in hers, and also with kisses, presents, and jewels; whereby he, despising the commands of God, and all human laws, 5 Nov. 27 Hen. VIII., violated and carnally knew the said Queen, his own sister, at Westminster; which he also did on divers other days before and after at the same place, sometimes by his own procurement and sometimes by the Queen's'.[33] Chapuys wrote,

> Her brother was charged with having cohabited with her by presumption, because he had been once found a long time with her, and with certain other little follies. To all he replied so well that several of those present wagered 10 to 1 that he would be acquitted, especially as no witnesses were produced against either him or her, as it is usual to do, particularly when the accused denies the charge.
>
> I must not omit, that among other things charged against him as a crime was, that his sister had told his wife that the King '*nestoit habile en cas de soy copuler avec femme, et quil navoit ne vertu ne puissance*'. This he was not openly charged with, but it was shown him in writing, with a warning not to repeat it. But he immediately declared the matter, in great

contempt of Cromwell and some others, saying he would not in this point arouse any suspicion which might prejudice the King's issue. He was also charged with having spread reports which called in question whether his sister's daughter was the King's child. To which he made no reply.[34]

To the chagrin of those betting on his acquittal, George was found guilty and sentenced to the grim traitor's death of hanging, drawing and quartering. He then stated that 'he would no longer maintain his innocence, but confessed that he had deserved death' – a standard admission for those who had been condemned to die, and not to be taken as a belated confession of guilt. George then asked that his debts be paid out of his goods, which as the result of his conviction would be forfeited to the crown.[35]

Chapuys wrote cheerfully, 'The joy shown by this people every day not only at the ruin of the Concubine but at the hope of the Princess' restoration, is inconceivable,' although he added, 'but as yet the King shows no great disposition towards the latter.'[36]

Two days after George and Anne's trial, on 17 May, the five condemned men, their sentences all commuted to beheading, were executed at Tower Hill. John Hussee informed Lord Lisle that they 'died very charitably'.[37] Chapuys claimed that it was arranged that Anne witness the executions from a vantage point at the Tower.[38] That afternoon at Lambeth Palace, the Archbishop of Canterbury pronounced Anne Boleyn's marriage to Henry VIII, which had cost so much to so many to procure, to have been invalid, on grounds that are now unknown. It may be that a precontract with Henry Percy, Earl of Northumberland, was the ground, although Northumberland, who had been in the unfortunate position of serving as one of the peers who condemned Anne to death, vehemently denied such a claim. Another possibility is the affair Henry had had with Anne's sister, Mary.[39] Whatever the reasons, the effect was to render Elizabeth illegitimate, like her older sister.

Meanwhile, Henry, as Chapuys reported, was wearing his cuckold's horns quite cheerfully.[40] 'I hear that on one occasion, returning by the river to Greenwich, the royal barge was actually filled with minstrels and musicians of his chamber, playing on all sorts of instruments or singing; which state of things was by many a one compared to the joy and pleasure a man feels in getting rid of a thin, old, and vicious hack in the hope of getting soon a fine horse to ride – a very peculiarly agreeable task for this king.' According to Chapuys, the king had even written a tragedy about his marriage, which he handed to the Bishop of Carlisle, who somehow managed to evade reading it. 'Perhaps these were certain ballads, which the King himself is known to have composed once, and of which the concubine and her brother had made fun, as of productions entirely worthless, which circumstance was one of the principal charges brought against them at the trial,' Chapuys surmised. Mary, in accordance with her new status as the king's senior illegitimate daughter, had been moved to better quarters, while Jane Seymour, 'splendidly entertained and served by cooks and officers of the royal household', was expected to become Henry's third queen.[41]

On 19 May, Anne walked to Tower Green, where a scaffold and a French swordsman awaited her. Antony Pickering, writing to Lady Lisle, estimated that about 1,000 people had crowded to see the spectacle of a king putting his queen to death.[42] The spectators included the Lord Chancellor, Thomas Cromwell, the king's illegitimate son, the Duke of Suffolk, most of the king's council, and unnamed earls, lords and nobles, as well as representatives from the London craft guilds,[43] so it is entirely likely that Henry and Geoffrey Pole were there to see the show as well. Anne did not disappoint. Clad in a damask gown and an ermine cloak and wearing an English headdress,[44] with a 'good and smiling countenance', Anne addressed the throng: 'Masters, I here humbly submit to the law as the law has judged me, and as for my offences, I accuse no man, God knoweth them; I remit them to God, beseeching him to have mercy on my soul, and I beseech Jesus save my sovereign and master the king, the most goodly, noble and gentle Prince that is, and long to reign over you.'[45]

As recorded by Hall, Anne added, 'If any person will meddle with my cause, I require them to judge the best.' Then, having bundled her hair into the cap supplied by her ladies, Anne knelt, tucked her skirts around her feet, and commended her soul to Jesus Christ, after which the executioner did his work 'before you could say a paternoster'. Hussee informed Lord Lisle that Anne had died 'boldly', and even Chapuys allowed, 'No one ever shewed more courage or greater readiness to meet death than she did.'[46]

Having learned of Anne's execution, Henry took a barge and paid a visit to Jane Seymour, lodged about a mile away. The next day, the couple were betrothed, and on 30 May they married.[47]

Even before Anne Boleyn's arrest, Jane, who according to Chapuys bore 'great love and reverence to the Princess', had reportedly urged Henry to restore Mary to her former position, only to receive a royal rebuff: '[T]he King told her she was a fool, and ought to solicit the advancement of the children they would have between them, and not any others. She replied that in asking for the restoration of the Princess she conceived she was seeking the rest and tranquillity of the King, herself, her future children, and the whole realm; for, without that, neither your Majesty nor this people would ever be content.'[48]

Now, with young Elizabeth deemed the bastard daughter of a disgraced queen, Mary seemed poised for a return to her father's favour. Accordingly, on 26 May, she wrote from her residence at Hunsdon to Cromwell, asking him to intervene with the king for her now that 'that woman', as Mary called Anne Boleyn, was gone.[49] A series of letters between Mary and Cromwell followed, after which the Duke of Norfolk and other councillors were sent to Hunsdon to demand that Mary submit to the king, which meant accepting him as supreme head of the Church and acknowledging that his marriage to Katherine of Aragon was invalid. If Mary had delusions that her father's ill-treatment of her was attributable solely to the malign influence of Anne Boleyn, they must have shattered at that moment. Nonetheless, she was her mother's daughter, and refused, to the fury and exasperation of Norfolk and his companions, who declared 'she was so unnatural as to oppose the King's will so obstinately, that they could scarcely believe she was his bastard, and if she was their daughter, they would beat her and knock her head so violently against the wall that they would make it as soft as baked apples, and that she was a traitress and should be punished, and several other words. And her gouvernante was commanded not to allow any one to speak to her, and that she and another should never lose sight of her day or night'.

Henry, according to Chapuys, was 'desperate with anger' when he heard of his daughter's intransigence, in part because he believed that she was being encouraged in her stubbornness by members of her household. (In this respect, it was fortunate for Margaret that she was no longer attendant upon Mary.) Cromwell, who had overestimated Mary's tractability, 'considered himself a dead man'. His fears were not idle, for Henry dismissed the Marquis of Exeter and Sir William Fitzwilliam from the Privy Council, imprisoned Lady Hussey, the wife of Mary's chamberlain, in the Tower, and ordered his judges to institute legal proceedings against his daughter. Cromwell, who aside from his fear of losing his head must have found the role of go-between between these two stubborn people to be highly distasteful, wrote to Mary to inform her, 'I think you the most obstinate and stubborn woman all things considered, that ever was', and to warn her that he would be of no more assistance to her if she persisted in her refusal. Chapuys, unwilling to make a martyr out of the young woman whose cause he had been championing for years, joined the chorus of voices urging Mary to submit to the king's will.

At last, Mary capitulated. The judges had delayed, suggesting that Mary be presented with a document to sign before any proceedings were taken against her, and on 22 June, Mary subscribed her name to it. She submitted herself to the king's authority, accepted him as supreme head of the Church of England, and – surely the provision that caused her the most agony – acknowledged that her mother's marriage to the king was 'incestuous and unlawful'. No wonder that after signing, Mary 'fell suddenly into a state of despondency and sorrow', which Chapuys attempted to relieve by telling her that 'not only will the Pope not condemn her action, but will highly approve of it under the circumstances'. Recognising the danger that had passed, Chapuys concluded gratefully, 'She never made a better day's work.'

9

AN OPINION GIVEN

Amid the rejoicing over Mary's submission, Margaret returned to court in late June, when, according to a 26 June letter by the Bishop of Faenza, she inadvertently caused a stir: 'On the return of [Margaret] to court, it being supposed that the Princess was in her company, a crowd with 4,000 or 5,000 horses ran to meet her.'[1] Margaret's stock had risen. The optimistic Lady Lisle, campaigning in June to get her daughter Anne Bassett a place in Jane Seymour's household, hastened to obtain the influence of Margaret, who 'made your ladyship's humble recommendations unto the Queen's highness, whose Grace was very glad to hear from your ladyship'. Margaret also advised that Lady Lisle attend Jane's coronation, an event that ultimately never took place. Lady Lisle was still enlisting both Margaret and her son Lord Montagu on her daughter's behalf in May 1537, when Lord Montagu advised Lord Lisle that 'my lady your bedfellow writ to me to speak to my lady my mother for a daughter of hers, in which you may be both assured I will do that may be in me. But and it please you to write a letter to my lady my mother yourself it will sooner take effect'.[2]

But if Margaret had hopes of resuming her place in Mary's life, these were soon to be dashed. The author of her disappointment was her own son.

In February 1535, Thomas Starkey, one of the king's chaplains, wrote to Reginald Pole at the king's command to ask Reginald's position on two questions: his opinion on the king's marriage and on the authority of the Pope. Two more dangerous questions can hardly be imagined, but Starkey, setting out his own arguments, made it clear that an answer which fell in line with the king's own thinking would be most satisfactory.[3]

Reginald was in no hurry to reply, and told Starkey that he would need time to reflect upon these questions. Nonetheless, he gave no sign that his ultimate answer would be anything other than what the king wanted to hear. Rather, he laid it on thick when he wrote to Cromwell in October 1535:

> I am informed by my Lord my brother's letters of the comfortable relation made by you of the continuance of the King's favor; which, though I am well assured I never deserved otherwise, I cannot but account a singular comfort, the time being such that I might have feared some alienation. Few of my friends could have done me such a benefit as this assurance gives me; and I beg you will do me the still greater favor to assure his Highness of my readiness to do him service at all times; for I count whatsoever is good in me next to God to proceed of his Grace's liberality in my education, which I esteem a greater benefit than all the promotions the King ever gave to any other.[4]

By the time he wrote this, however, Reginald had already begun composing his reply to the king. It was not one intended to do his Highness service.

Reginald finally sent his reply, in the form of a book entitled *Pro ecclesiasticae unitatis defensione* (*Defence of the unity of the church*, known more familiarly as *De unitate*), in May 1536. With passages addressed to Henry such as 'You have squandered a huge treasure; you have made a laughing-stock of the nobility; you have never loved the people; you have pestered and robbed the clergy in every possible way; and lately you have destroyed the best men of your kingdom, not like a human being, but a wild beast', it was not calculated to please the king – nor did it.[5] A further taste of the book's contents can be gleaned from this abstract:

After expressing the difficulty he has in writing either against the King or against his own conscience, seeing that others have been punished with death for their loyalty, he says he nevertheless feels it a duty, as he is the only one of the English nobility whom the King has educated from a boy ... Speaks of the execution of Fisher and More, and of More's character as a judge, of his trial, and of his daughter embracing him on the way to execution,—how he was seen looking grey for the first time on coming out of prison, and how even strangers could not refrain from tears on hearing of his fate. Pole himself can hardly write for tears, having known the man as he did. Describes also Fisher's character, and refers to the Carthusian and Bridgetine martyrs, especially to one whom he knew personally, by name Reynolds, remarkable for his holiness of life and for his learning. He was the only monk in England who knew the three languages. Such was his constancy that, as an eyewitness informed Pole, he put his own neck into the noose, looking more like one putting on the insignia of royalty than one about to undergo punishment. Refers also to the Observants. Though it seems a hopeless task to recall Henry to virtue, yet as the prayers of Mary and Martha recalled a brother from corruption, so Katharine now prays for her husband, and Mary for her father; even Achab repented. Compares Henry's conduct to that of Nero and Domitian, and appeals to the Emperor to protect thousands of Christians from a far greater danger than the Turk. At the very time of Charles V's glorious expedition to Africa, Henry, bearing most untruly the name of Defender of the Faith, did not merely kill but tore to pieces all the true defenders of old religion in a more inhuman fashion than the Turk. Who that knew Fisher would have expected that a man so old and feeble in health and slender in body could have endured imprisonment even for one month? Pole, certainly, when he left England three years before, did not believe that, with the utmost care, he would have lived more than a year longer. Was told afterwards that when he was brought to London to be sent to prison he was so weak that for some time he lost consciousness. Yet he endured 15 months' imprisonment. 'Who,' the writer asks, 'does not acknowledge the hand of God beyond nature that lengthened his life to your shame that he might perish by your sword, and allowed him to be enrolled among the number of cardinals, that it might be known to the whole world that you had slain not merely an excellent bishop, against whom you had no just cause, but a cardinal over whom you had no authority?' The writer then warns the King that the Pope is urgently entreated to expel him from the Church as a rotten member, nor can Henry expect his subjects to keep faith with him when he has broken it so shamefully with them. During the 27 years he has reigned he has continually plundered them, and if he was liberal in anything, it was certainly not in things making for the common weal. He has robbed every kind of man, made a sport of the nobility, never loved the people, troubled the clergy, and torn like a wild beast the men who were the greatest honor to his kingdom. What epitaph is to be placed on Henry's tomb except the recital of these facts, unless this is to be added, that he has obtained for himself from the universities the name of an incestuous person, and by the slaughter of his best men has got himself acknowledged 'Head of the Church.' Warns him by the fate of Richard III, that he may find few friends one day, and concludes with a strong exhortation to repentance.[6]

There were more offensive comparisons Reginald could have made than comparing a Tudor king to Richard III, but it is hard to think of very many.

What was the cause of such invective? Henry had always been generous to Reginald Pole, and while Reginald's mother had been a casualty of Henry's fraught relationships with his daughter Mary and his first queen, her removal from Mary's household hardly justified such a tirade. Wilhelm Schenk's explanation is that Reginald, having 'worshipped' the king (Pole's word), became just as violently disenchanted when Henry ordered the executions of Sir Thomas More and Cardinal Fisher.[7]

But Reginald did not content himself with merely haranguing Henry. He raised the touchy subject of his own royal blood by declaring the innocence of his uncle, Edward, Earl of Warwick; he predicted dire consequences for the realm if Henry repudiated his daughter Mary; and he invited Charles V to invade England.[8]

Margaret soon had the dubious privilege of hearing this from the king himself, who received Reginald's book at about the same time Mary capitulated to the king and Margaret came to court. As Margaret recalled later, following what must have been a distinctly uncomfortable meeting with Henry, Margaret sent for her son Lord Montagu, who advised her to inform her servants that she regarded Reginald as a traitor. This Margaret did: 'She took her said son for a traitor and for no son, and that she would never take him otherwise.'[9]

But the matter did not end there. At the king's urging, Margaret wrote to her son. As abstracted, her letter reads:

'Son Reginald,' I send you God's blessing and mine, though my trust to have comfort in you is turned to sorrow. Alas that I, for your folly, should receive from my sovereign lord 'such message as I have late done by your brother.' To me as a woman, his Highness has shown such mercy and pity as I could never deserve, but that I trusted my children's services would express my duty. And now, to see you in his Grace's indignation,—'trust me, Reginald, there went never the death of thy father or of any child so nigh my heart.' Upon my blessing I charge thee to take another way and serve our master, as thy duty is, unless thou wilt be the confusion of thy mother. You write of a promise made by you to God,—'Son, that was to serve God and thy prince, whom if thou do not serve with all thy wit, with all thy power, I know thou cannot please God. For who hath brought you up and maintained you to learning but his Highness?' Will pray God to give him grace to serve his prince truly or else to take him to his mercy.[10]

Lord Montagu, writing from Bisham on 13 September, addressed his brother, who was journeying to Rome, in yet stronger terms:

I perceive by your letter of 15 July that you remember the unkindness I reckoned in you when your sentence was required in the King's matter, and that now you fear I would take more displeasure. I knew nothing of the effect of your book when I received your letter, which made me greatly to doubt what before I had hoped for. To be out of doubt, spoke with the Lord Privy Seal, to whom you are as much bound as if you were his near kinsman. He advised me to speak with the King, but said nothing himself. At time convenient spoke with the King, who declared a great part of your book so at length that it made my poor heart so to lament that if I had lost mother, wife, and children it could no more have done, for that had been but natural. But you, to show yourself so unnatural to so noble a prince, of whom you cannot deny next God you have received all things. And for our family, which was clean trodden under foot, he set up nobly, which showeth his charity, his clemency, and his mercy.

I grieve to see the day that you should set forth the contrary, or trust to your wit above the rest of the country, whose mind you will perceive from him whom you bade read your book. If there is any grace in you, now you will turn to the right way, and then we may reckon it was the will of God that your ingratitude should show the King's meekness. He has borne your slanders more patiently than the poorest in the country could do, and is contented that your friends should instruct you of what moves them, as I know those who are learned have done. I, who lack learning, could never conceive that laws made by man were of such strength but that they might be undone again by man, for what seems politic at one time, by abusion proves at another time the contrary. Therefore, gentle Reginald, let no scrupulosity so embrace your stomach but that we, which be so knit in nature and so happily born under so noble a prince, may so join together to serve him, as our bounden duties requireth. It is incredible to me that by reason of a brief sent to you from the bishop of Rome you should be resident with him this winter. If you should take that way, then fare well all my hope. Learning you may well have, but doubtless no prudence nor pity, but showeth yourself to run from one mischief to another. And then farewell all bonds of nature, not only of me, but of all mine, or else instead of my blessing they shall have my curse. But utterly out of hope I cannot be that ever superstition should so reign in you that you would so highly offend God to lose the benefits of so noble a prince, your native country, and whole family, without the devil have so much power over you, from the which to keep you I shall as heartily pray, as I would be partner of the joys of Heaven, which Christ make us partakers of.[11]

Reginald remained obdurate to his mother's and his brother's pleas. Writing to Margaret on 15 July, he reminded her that she had given him 'utterly unto God' and should therefore 'commit all to His goodness, as I doubt not your ladyship will, and shall be to me the greatest comfort I can have of you'.[12] Later, he declared to a correspondent, 'The king well knows how much I love my family, and tried to use them to sway me by writing letters which accused me of renouncing my king. Told them I had another and that if I lost them, would have the love of the martyrs.'[13]

Mary, meanwhile, was reassembling her household, albeit on a modest scale. Margaret was not included.[14] As Hazel Pierce points out,[15] this may have been in part because Mary, now twenty, no longer needed a governess; moreover, no other noblewomen were in the new household. But Mary, having undergone an uneasy reconciliation with her father after submitting to his will, may also have not wished to risk the wrath of the king now that Margaret was so deeply compromised by her son Reginald's activities.

Henceforth, Margaret spent most of her time at her manor of Warblington.[16] Surrounded by her eleven ladies, five of whom were her granddaughters (see Chapter 4), Margaret, now sixty-three, might well have been content to return to her own estates, far from the tumultuous (and expensive) court. She maintained contact with Mary, sending her New Year's gifts in 1537 and 1538 (New Year's being the gift-giving holiday at that time), for which her servants were duly rewarded by the princess with fifteen shillings in 1537 and twenty shillings in 1538.[17]

Meanwhile, in October 1536, disaffected northerners, whose grievances included the Dissolution of the Monasteries and Henry's religious changes, had risen against the king in the so-called Pilgrimage of Grace. There were the familiar calls for the expulsion of low-born councillors (e.g., Cromwell) and the demand that Mary be recognised as the king's legitimate daughter and his heir. As dissent raged in England, Reginald Pole was made a cardinal in December 1536. The Pope then appointed him legate, with hopes that he could persuade either King Francis of France or Emperor Charles to assist the English rebels. By this time, though, the rebellion had been suppressed, and neither king nor emperor was inclined to make an enemy of Henry at that time. Thus, as David Loades notes, Reginald's 'mission was a complete waste of time. What it did do was to convince Henry that Reginald was a double-dyed traitor.'[18]

The next October started out as a much better one for King Henry: Jane Seymour gave birth to his hoped-for heir, Edward. Margaret played no role at the prince's christening, but her family was represented by Lord Montagu. He supported the Earl of Sussex, who carried in a pair of covered basins.[19] Soon Montagu was compelled to perform a sadder duty when Jane fell victim to childbed fever, a common killer of new mothers. At her funeral, held on 12 November 1537, he and the Lord Clifford assisted Mary, who was the queen's chief mourner.[20] As he took his place in the procession beside Mary, who rode upon a horse trapped in black velvet, he could have hardly guessed that the next burial he attended, thirteen months later, would be his own.

IO

COMING TO STRIPES

In June 1538, Hugh Holland, a servant of Geoffrey Pole and an erstwhile pirate, was arrested. Six months later, he and five other people would be dead, three by beheading and three by hanging. A seventh person, Margaret, would die on the block three years later.

Ironically, it may have been Margaret's pious act of maintaining a 'surgeon house' near Warblington that set in motion the chain of events that destroyed her.[1] Richard Ayer, the house surgeon, believed that Margaret kept 'a company of priests [in her] house which did her much harm and kept her [from] the true knowledge of God's word' – the burgeoning 'New Learning' which Ayer seems to have embraced. Margaret, Ayer claimed, knew all of the county's business, for the local priests broke the sanctity of the confessional – including an indignant Ayer's – and told her what their penitents had said.

Gervase Tyndall was a schoolmaster with ties to Thomas Cromwell, Henry's Lord Privy Seal. He turned up in Hampshire in the summer of 1538 and lodged at the hospital, apparently on a spying mission for Cromwell, who had his own connections in Hampshire and may have heard disquieting rumours about the Pole family's loyalty, or lack thereof. The disgruntled Ayer was more than happy to chat with his lodger, informing him that Holland was conveying letters to Reginald Pole and that 'all the secrets of the realm of England [were] known to the bishop of Rome as well as though he were here'.

Meanwhile, according to Tyndall, Margaret, suspecting that he was of the New Learning, ordered Ayer to send him away. Tyndall refused to go until his supposedly poor health had improved, whereupon Margaret ordered Ayer to send all of the patients away, a decision Ayer attributed to Margaret's gang of priests. Before she gave this order, however, the helpful Ayer had referred Tyndall to a man named Peter, identified by Hazel Pierce as possibly Peter Wythends, who claimed that Margaret's council had refused to allow Margaret's tenants to possess the English-language New Testament or other books that enjoyed the king's approval. For the time being, however, the government was more interested in Holland, who was duly arrested.

In custody, Holland gave damning evidence against Geoffrey Pole, some of it linked to Margaret's chaplain, John Helyar, who had left the country in 1534, incurring the disapproval of the Bishop of Winchester, who wrote on 26 July that Helyar had left 'in such fashion as I like not'.[2] Helyar, it turned out, was strongly opposed to Henry VIII's religious changes and had fled England for fear of being put to death, departing in secret because Margaret would not give him leave. This had not stopped Geoffrey from corresponding with him, however.

This was nothing, however, compared to what came next, at least as Holland told it. When Holland went to Flanders to sell some wheat, Geoffrey asked him to deliver a message to Reginald in which Geoffrey offered to join his brother. He then gave his opinion that 'the world in England waxes all crooked, God's law is turned upside down, abbeys and churches overthrown and he [Reginald] is taken for a traitor', and claimed that hired assassins had been sent to dispatch Reginald. When Holland met Reginald, the latter sent a message to Margaret, recalling 'that she and I looking upon a wall together read this, *Spea mea in deo est* ['My hope is in God], and desire her blessing for me. I trust she will be glad of mine also.' Should Margaret share the negative opinions of others about Reginald, however, her son said, 'mother as she is mine, I would tread upon her with my feet'. For Geoffrey, Reginald had the sage advice to 'meddle little and let all things alone'. Disregarding this, Geoffrey continued to talk of going overseas, where he hoped to kiss the Pope's foot. Instead, on 29 August 1538, he was arrested and sent to the Tower, where Holland was already residing.

The sentiments Geoffrey allegedly expressed to Holland were not new ones. Chapuys had reported to Charles in 1534:

> The state of things in this kingdom is such that should Your Majesty send the smallest possible force, all the people would at once declare in your favour, especially if the said Seigneur Reynard [Reginald Pole] were in the country. The latter's younger brother [Geoffrey] is with me, and would visit me almost every day, had I not dissuaded him from doing so, on account of the danger he might run. He, however, ceases not, like many others, to importune and beg me to write to Your Majesty, and explain how very easy the conquest of this kingdom would be, and that the inhabitants are only waiting for a signal. I have never spoken to him about his brother, except warning him that the latter had much better remain where he is now, and beg his daily bread in the streets, than attempt returning here in these troubled times, for fear he should be treated as the poor bishop of Rochester, or worse still. This he assures me he has done, having written to him many a time, and made his mother also write and warn him not to come here.[3]

Geoffrey Pole remained in the Tower for two months before finally being interrogated formally. Asked to name those with whom he had discussed 'a change of this world' – that is, a regime change – he named several people, including his own brother, Lord Montagu, although he hastened to add that Montagu no longer retained his former enthusiasm for changing the world and that in any case, the change referred to religious matters, not to the king's person. None of this lessened the government's interest in Lord Montagu and the rest, and Geoffrey, an amicable man with a fondness for puns and a weakness for getting into debt, realised he was hopelessly out of his depth. So miserable and guilt-stricken was he, and perhaps threatened with torture as well, that he made a suicide attempt. John Hussee reported to Lord Lisle on 28 October that Geoffrey was 'so in despair that he would have murdered himself and, as it was told me, hurt himself sore', and Richard Morisyne claimed that he stabbed himself in the chest with a blunt knife.[4] Nonetheless, the interrogations, and the revelations, continued, with Geoffrey implicating Gertrude, Marchioness of Exeter, and banging nail after nail into his brother's coffin. Montagu, he said, had predicted that 'suddenly his leg will kill [the king] and then we shall have jolly stirring'. Geoffrey also claimed that Lord Montagu had said that one day the King would go so far that all the world would mislike him, and that when the king had told his lords he would be gone one day, Montagu had sneered, 'If he will serve us so, we shall be happily rid.' Montagu maintained that he had never loved the king and that the king would eventually go out of his wits.

Jerome Ragland, Montagu's 'right hand', corroborated some of Geoffrey's evidence against Montagu and added some of his own. He agreed that when the king, in a fit of pique, told the lords that he would 'forsake them and go with the Lubekks', Montagu had said that they would be well rid of him. According to Ragland, Montagu, if sent overseas, would want to remain there until the country was in a better estate, and he had speculated, presumably optimistically, that Henry 'could not long continue with his sore leg'. Ragland also assured his interrogators that Lord Montagu and the Marquis of Exeter were good friends. All of this ensured that on 4 November, both Montagu and Exeter were arrested, followed at some point by their young sons and by Exeter's wife. Sir Edward Neville, whose choice remarks included the sally that 'his highness was a beast and worse than a beast', and who enjoyed singing tunes to the effect that the 'world would amend and that honest men should rule one day', made the trip to the Tower on 5 November. Presently, they were joined by John Collins, who was Montagu's chaplain and who had predicted that the king and Cromwell would 'hang in hell' for the dissolution of the monasteries, and by George Croftes, chancellor of Chichester Cathedral, who after taking the Oath of Supremacy recognizing Henry as the head of the Church of England had groused that 'none act or thing that ever he did more grieved his conscience'.

Unlike his younger brother, Lord Montagu kept his nerve while in prison, revealing little of an incriminating nature but admitting that he had burned letters. So unforthcoming was he that he was interrogated only once.

All this time, Margaret had been at Warblington, from which in September she had written to advise Montagu 'both in word and deed to serve your prince not disobeying God's commandments as far as your power and life will serve you'. Her comptroller and receiver general, Oliver Frankelyn, recalled that after Geoffrey made his suicide attempt, Frankelyn had told Margaret that he prayed that Geoffrey would do her no harm because he had the feeling that 'the said Sir Geoffrey should one day turn her to displeasure'. According to Frankelyn, Margaret had made the cool reply, 'I trow he is not so unhappy that he will hurt his mother, and yet I care neither for him, nor for any other, for I am true to my Prince.' Yet the events swirling around Margaret had not entirely overshadowed her daily preoccupations as a great lady, for in that same September, Sir Antony Windsor told Lord Lisle that Margaret was 'very desirous' of obtaining Lord Lisle's lease of Soberton.

Now it was time for Margaret to face her own ordeal, however. On 12 November 1538, William Fitzwilliam, Earl of Southampton, and Thomas Goodrich, Bishop of Ely, arrived at Warblington to question Margaret. Over two days, with the fates of her two sons and their friends hanging in the balance, she withstood sharp questioning. Asked whether Reginald Pole had confided in her that he was going overseas because he disliked the way the kingdom was governed and that he had left her a token beginning with the words '*spes mea*', Margaret replied that not only had Reginald not discussed the king's statutes or proceedings with her, but that she had not wished for him to go abroad. The motto '*spes mea*' was a 'common word written in the windows and other places of the house'. She had not received any letter concerning Reginald except one from the king himself, and she had neither consented nor known about Hugh Holland being sent to see Reginald.

Margaret acknowledged that Geoffrey had told her that the king was planning to assassinate Reginald, and that 'she prayed God heartily to change the king's mind. And being examined who told her that the cardinal had escaped that danger, she says both her sons; and for motherly pity she could not but rejoice.' Asked whether she had heard that Lord Montagu and Geoffrey Pole were planning to join Reginald, Margaret responded that she 'pray[ed] God she may be torn in pieces if ever she heard such a thing of her sons'. She denied wishing, along with her sons, that Reginald 'should be Pope one day and come into England again', but, rather poignantly, acknowledged that she had 'often wished to see him again in England with the King's favour, though he were but a poor parish priest'. She 'utterly denie[d] having conversations with her sons wherein they lamented the King's proceedings and wished for a change'. She acknowledged that she was sorry for the destruction of the abbeys and houses of religion where her ancestors lay, but was more concerned with the strife concerning the living. She had never heard Lord Montagu claiming that 'none ruled about the King but knaves'.

Asked whether she and her sons had agreed to burn their letters from Reginald and from the Exeters when they learned of Hugh Holland's arrest, Margaret replied that she had never burned any letter concerning the king, only 'private men's letters of small importance', and she had not heard of her sons burning letters. She had not received any treasonous messages from the Marquis of Exeter or his wife. Margaret had never heard her son say that 'this world was turned upside down, or that it would come to stripes, or that she ever heard her son wish or look for the King's death' or any of the other compromising words attributed to him. Margaret did admit that Geoffrey Pole had gone overseas to Guisnes without her knowledge or that of Lord Montagu until the latter forced him to return; had Montagu not succeeded, she added, Geoffrey would have 'gone in warfare', although Margaret did not know with whom.

Margaret was vehement when asked again whether Montagu and Geoffrey wanted to join Reginald overseas: 'she denieth utterly her baptism and prayeth that she never see God in the face if ever she heard any such words'. Questioned about whether Lord Montagu had complained that Lord Darcy, the leader of the Pilgrimage of Grace, had 'played the fool going about to pluck away the Council for he should have gone about to pluck away the head', she answered 'upon her damnation' that she had never heard him say such a thing.

Margaret confirmed that Oliver Frankelyn had warned her that Geoffrey might 'one day will do you a displeasure'. Requested to elaborate, Frankelyn had predicted that Geoffrey would slip away, to which Margaret had replied, 'Nay, he will not be so unhappy.'

As the interview dragged to a close, Margaret recalled her meeting with the king following his receipt of Reginald's letter.

When she spoke with the King his Grace he showed her how her son had written against him. 'Alas ... thy what grief is this to me to see him whom ... set up to be so ungracious and unhappy.' And up[on th]is when her son Montague came home to her ... she said to him 'What hath the King shown me of [my] son? Alas, son, said she, what a child have I [in] him:' And then my lord Montague [counseled her] to declare him us a traitor to their servan[ts], that they might so report him when they came in to their countries. And so she called her servants and declared unto them accordingly. She took her said son for a traitor and for no son, and that she would never take him otherwise.[5]

Having given her statements, Margaret signed her name at the bottom of each page.

It had been a gruelling interview for all concerned. Margaret's interrogators, writing to Cromwell on 14 November, groused, 'Yesterday ... we travailed with the Lady of Salisbury all day, both before and after noon, till almost night. Albeit for all we could do, though we used her diversely, she would utter and confess little or nothing more than the first day.' Despite being 'entreated in both sorts, sometime with ... mild words, now roughly ... by traitoring her and her sons to the ninth degree, yet will she nothing utter, but maketh herself clear, and as unspotted, utterly denies all that is objected unto her; and that with most stiff and earnest words'. The men concluded that 'either her sons have not made her privy nor participant of the bottom and pit [of] their stomachs, or else is she the [most] errant traitoress that ever [lived]'.

Having learned little of value from Margaret, the Earl of Southampton and the Bishop of Ely decided to seize Margaret's goods and move the unhelpful countess to Southampton's manor of Cowdray, a proceeding at which the countess appeared, not surprisingly, to be 'somewhat appalled'. This move, they hoped, might motivate Margaret to 'utter somewhat'.[6] The earl and the bishop had underestimated Margaret, however. In dismay, they wrote to Cromwell, '[W]e have dealt with such a one, as men have not dealt withal before us; we may call her rather a strong and constant man, than a woman. For in all behaviour howsoever we have used her, she has showed herself so earnest, vehement, and precise, that more could not be.'[7]

But despite Margaret's intransigence, the investigation was proceeding along nicely from the Crown's point of view, as other witnesses were more forthcoming. Just two weeks later, Lord Montagu was tried before a jury of his peers at Westminster Hall on 2 December, followed by the Marquess of Exeter on 3 December and Geoffrey Pole, Edward Neville, Hugh Holland, George Croftes and John Collins on 4 December. The indictment of Lord Montagu recited choice utterances such as, 'I like well the doings of my brother the Cardinal, and I would we were both over the sea, for this world will one day come to stripes. It must needs to come to pass one day; and I fear me we shall lack nothing so much as honest men'; '[The king] is not dead, but he will die one day suddenly. His leg will kill him, and then we shall have jolly stirring'; 'The King said to the lords that he should go from them one day. If he will serve us so we shall be happily rid. I never loved him from childhood'; 'He will be out of his wit one day'; 'Knaves rule about the King. I trust the world will amend, and that we shall have a day upon these knaves. And this world will come to stripes one day'; and 'Cardinal Wolsey had been an honest man if he had had an honest master'. Exeter was accused of meeting with Montagu and uttering similar sentiments, including the remark, uttered with a clenched fist, 'Knaves rule about the king. I trust to give them a buffet one day.' Geoffrey's ill-advised remarks consisted of 'Brother, I like well the proceedings of my brother Reginald Pole, cardinal at Rome; but I like not the doings and proceedings in this realm, and I trust to see a change of this world'; 'Commend me to my brother, the cardinal Pole, and show him I would I were with him, and I will come to him, if he will have me, to show him the world in England waxeth all crooked, God's law is turned upside down, abbeys and churches overthrown, and he is taken for a traitor, and I think they will cast down parish churches and all at the last. And because he shall trust you, show him this token, and show him further that there been men sent from England daily to destroy him, and that much money would be given for his head.'[8]

Exeter and Montagu were each tried by twenty-eight of their fellow noblemen, the rest before a commission of oyer and terminer. By the standards of the day, the trials were fair, with no signs of rigging. Unanimously, the men were found guilty and were sentenced to the traditional traitor's death of hanging, drawing and quartering. As was also traditional, the higher-ranking – Montagu, Exeter and Neville – had their sentences commuted to the gentlemanly death by beheading. Croftes, Collins and Holland suffered the complete ordeal at Tyburn on 9 December 1538, with their heads sent to

London Bridge and their quarters placed 'on divers gates about London' as a reminder of the price of treason. That same day, immediately after the Tyburn executions, Montagu, Exeter and Neville lost their heads at Tower Green. They were spared the indignity of the public display of their bodies, which were buried along with their heads at the Tower's Chapel of Vincula, where Anne Boleyn had been buried in 1536.[9] Geoffrey was pardoned on 2 January 1539. Two days later, according to Chapuys, he made a second attempt at self-destruction: 'I am told his life is granted to him, but he must remain in perpetual prison; also that on the 4th day of the feasts he tried to suffocate himself with a cushion.'[10]

Before we leave Geoffrey to his guilt and misery, we must ask: were these executions justified? The popular view, little questioned until recently, was that Lord Montagu, Exeter and the rest were victims of an abuse of power on Cromwell's part and/ or Henry VIII's desire to rid himself of his Yorkist cousins with potential claims to the throne. As Hazel Pierce, John Schofield and David Loades have each pointed out, however, this is far too simplistic a view.[11] Since 1352, 'to compass or imagine the death of the king' was held to be treason, as was to 'adhere to the king's enemies and be provably attaint of it by men of the offender's own condition'. As noted in Chapter 7, in 1534, Henry VIII's Parliament had enacted legislation which made it treason to 'wish or attempt bodily harm to the king, queen or the royal heir by malicious deeds, writings and spoken words', as well as to call the king 'in writing or by spoken word a heretic, a schismatic, a tyrant, an infidel or an usurper of the crown'.[12] The condemned's words, reported by numerous witnesses whose accounts corroborate each other, fell neatly within both statutes. Only the most quiescent government could have ignored such talk, particularly with the possibility of French or imperial interference in England's affairs, urged on by Reginald Pole and his allies within England. Henry VIII, after all, owed his throne to his father's French-supported invasion of England. As for Henry's trying to rid himself of his Yorkist rivals, Henry had welcomed his cousins at his court and raised Margaret to the peerage, hardly the acts of one hell-bent on eradicating his Plantagenet rivals. Indeed, had that been his purpose in 1538, it is hard to see why Geoffrey Pole was left alive, along with his sons, who would later cause trouble during Elizabeth's reign.

Before the executions, Robert Warner had written to Robert Ratcliffe, Lord Fitzwalter, 'My lady Marquess is in the Tower, and my lady of Salisbury is in hold, as I heard my lord say, but where I cannot tell, but there is like to be a foul work among them.'[13] In fact, bereaved of her oldest son, Margaret remained at Cowdray in the custody of Southampton, who was busily searching through her coffers even after the executions. On 16 December, he found some money and her will, which Margaret had prudently made in September 1538, preparing for the worst. Dutifully forwarding the document to Cromwell, Southampton discovered a second document, cut in half, and questioned Margaret about it. Margaret explained that this was her previous will, made ten years before, and that 'when she made her new will, she cut her name from the old to utterly to damn it'.[14]

With her eldest son lying headless in a traitor's grave and her youngest son a shattered creature, her anguish can easily be imagined. But Margaret nonetheless managed to spar with her host, as he described to Cromwell in a letter dated 14 March 1539:

Because my wife since her coming hither has not seen my lady of Sarum [Salisbury], nor I, since my first coming, repaired to her, she takes it grievously; inasmuch that a gentleman of mine, who does nothing but attend on her, told me she besought me to speak with her. I went this afternoon and showed her I and my wife could not find it in our hearts to see her when 'that arrant whoreson traitor, her son the Cardinal, went about from prince to prince' to work trouble to the King and realm. She replied with a wonderful sorrowful countenance that though he were an ill man to behave so to the King who had been so good to him, yet was he no whoreson, for she was both a good woman and true. She wished he were in Heaven or that she could bring him to the King's presence, and she hoped the King would not impute his heinous offence to her. I had no further talk with her, nor will while I am here. I beg you to rid me of her company, for she is both chargeable and troubles my mind. I send a few Shelsay cockles.[15]

A few days afterward, on 20 March, a relieved Southampton wrote to Cromwell to tell him that his wife was pleased that Cromwell had agreed to help relieve her of the countess: 'I was fain to take her with me to Portsmouth, for in nowise would she tarry behind me, the said lady being in my house.' Perhaps the 'Shelsay cockles' had moved Cromwell in Southampton's favour, for he sent more, albeit with the proviso that they were 'not quite so good as they would be at the full of the moon'.[16]

Whether Margaret was sent to another private home or to the Tower at this point is unknown, but her situation was becoming more grim every day, for in May 1539, Parliament attainted her of treason – a mechanism which avoided having to give her a trial as her son Montagu had had. The evidence against her appears to have been quite vague, which was undoubtedly why the government chose this means of proceeding. Margaret was attainted in company with the Marchioness of Exeter, who was accused of assisting Nicholas Carew, who had been arrested following the executions of Montagu and the others and had been beheaded in February 1539.[17] Margaret's own attainder reads:

And where also Margaret Pole, Countess of Salisbury, and Hugh Vaughan, late of Beckener, in the County of Monmouth, yeoman, by instigation of the devil, putting apart the dread of Almighty God, their duty of allegiance, and the excellent benefit received of his Highness, have not only traitorously confederated themselves with the false and abominable traitors Henry Pole, Lord Montagu, and Reginald Pole, sons to the said countess, knowing them to be false traitors, but also have maliciously aided, abetted, maintained, and comforted them in their said false and abominable treason, to the most fearful peril of his HIghness, the commonwealth of this realm, &c., the said marchioness and the said countess be declared attainted, and shall suffer the pains and penalties of high treason.[18]

After the Act of Attainder was read, Cromwell is said to have displayed 'in profound silence' a tunic taken from Margaret's coffers.[19] John Worth, writing to Margaret's cousin Arthur, Viscount Lisle, on 18 May 1539, explained:

[T]here was a coat-armour found in the [Countess] of Salisbury's coffer, and by the one side of the coat there was the King's Grace his arms of England, that is, the lions without the flower de luce, and about the whole arms was made pansies for Pole, and marigolds for my Lady Mary. This was about the coat armour. And betwixt the marigold and the pansy was made a tree to rise in the midst; and on the tree a coat of purple hanging on a bough, in tokening of the coat of Christ; and on the other side of the coat all the Passion of Christ. Pole intended to have married my Lady Mary, and betwixt them both should again arise the old doctrine of Christ. This was the intent that the coat was made, as it is openly known in the Parliament house, as Master Sir George Speke shewed me. And this my Lady Marquess, my Lady Salisbury ... with divers others are attainted today by act of Parliament.[20]

The news of Margaret's attainder soon reached her son Reginald, who wrote in September 1539, 'You have heard, I believe, of my mother being condemned to death by public council, or rather, to eternal life. Not only has he who condemned her, condemned a woman of seventy, than whom he has no near relation except his daughter, and of whom he used to say there was no holier woman in his Kingdom; but, at the same time, her grandson, son of my brother, a child, the remaining hope of our race.'[21]

Not everyone, however, was distressed at Margaret's fate. A person who was attainted lost his or her estates, which then became ripe for the picking by those who could gain access to the right ear. Sir Ralph Ellerkar was not a man to miss such an opportunity. On 19 June 1539, he wrote to Cromwell, 'As I hear all the lands that were lady Salisbury's will come to the King, I beg you will get me the manor of Cottyngam.'[22]

The vultures were circling.

THE LADY IN THE TOWER

By 20 November 1539, and probably well before that, Margaret was a prisoner in the Tower, as shown by a roster of its inmates. Her grandson Henry was still there, along with the Marchioness of Exeter and her son Edward Courtenay.[1] The next month, a keeper at the Tower, Thomas Phillips, asked Cromwell for additional clothing for the two ladies in his charge, as well as their attendants. After detailing the marchioness's lack of clothing, he concluded, 'the Lady Salisbury maketh great moan for that she wanteth necessary apparel both for to change and also to keep her warm'.[2]

Phillips had also conveyed the marchioness's distress at standing 'in displeasure of the king's most gracious highness' and her desire to obtain Cromwell's favour. In this she was apparently successful, for on 21 December 1539 she was pardoned and released, although the twelve-year-old Edward Courtenay remained in the Tower; the following year, the king granted her £100, followed by an annuity.[3] As Sarah Donelson points out, Gertrude Courtenay represented little threat to the Crown, with her husband dead and her only son, a minor, shut up in the Tower. Margaret, by contrast, was the mother of Reginald Pole, a traitor still quite capable of stirring up trouble abroad.[4] She would stay put in the Tower. In the meantime, commissioners seeing to the dissolution of Christchurch priory, having found Margaret's intended resting place there, reported on

2 December that they had defaced it and destroyed Margaret's arms, although the magnificent structure, empty of a body, remains.[5]

Little is known about Margaret's days in the Tower. The king provided £13 6s 8d a month for her, her grandson and Edward Courtenay, plus eighteen shillings per week for a woman to wait upon Margaret. In March 1541, the Privy Council ordered Scutte, the queen's tailor, to make clothing for Margaret: a furred nightgown; a worsted kirtle; a furred petticoat; a gown in the fashion of a nightgown, lined with satin and faced with satin; a bonnet with a frontlet; four pairs of hose; four pairs of shoes; and one pair of slippers.[6] A 'night gown' was not a garment for sleeping, but a loose gown used both indoors and outdoors by both sexes; its comparative informality would have made it an appropriate garment for one imprisoned in the Tower.[7] By now the king had moved on to a fifth queen, Katherine Howard. It is sometimes claimed that she arranged for the clothing to be bought for the elderly, chilly countess,[8] but there is no evidence of Katherine's involvement. As clothing was ordered at the same time for Arthur, Viscount Lisle, now a prisoner himself, it seems that these were routine expenditures rather than the product of queenly intercession.[9]

Margaret, however, was not destined to enjoy her new clothing for long. On 27 May 1541, the countess was beheaded in a secluded part of the Tower.

* * *

Why execute the countess, who at age sixty-seven could have been permitted to die of natural causes in her prison? As Hazel Pierce points out, it was most likely a convergence of events in the winter and spring of 1541 that made Henry decide to carry out the death sentence under which Margaret had lain since 1539.[10] First, in January 1541, the king's ambassador Thomas Wyatt was arrested and accused of having had 'intelligence with the King's traitor Pole'; the following month, another ambassador, Sir John Wallop, was placed in custody. During this period, Anne Ragland, who had once served Margaret, was questioned about burning letters after the arrest of Lord Montagu, while John Babham, Margaret's former steward, had been questioned about a week before Wyatt's arrest. Second, a rising was brewing in the always restless, religiously conservative north. One of the leaders was Sir John Neville of Chevet, perhaps a distant relation of Margaret's Neville mother. Third, in an undated letter to the Bishop of Lavaur, Reginald Pole alluded to plans to free his mother from the Tower, although as Pierce points out, it is unknown whether Henry VIII was aware of them. It also appears that Henry, who was preparing to go north on a progress, was doing some house cleaning: Marillac, the French ambassador, wrote on 29 May that 'before St. John's tide, they reckon to empty the Tower of the prisoners now there for treason'. At the end of June, he reported, 'Before his departure [the king] has given order for the Tower to be cleared of prisoners, and, as he lately began by the execution of the countess of Salisbury ... such progress has since been made that in eight days all will be despatched, either by condemnation or absolution.'[11]

In his account of Margaret's execution, Marillac, referring to her death as 'a case more worthy of compassion than of long letters', wrote that Margaret 'was yesterday morning, about 7 o'clock, beheaded in a corner of the Tower, in presence of so few people that until evening the truth was still doubted. It was the more difficult to believe as she had been long prisoner, was of noble lineage, above 80 years old, and had been punished by the loss of one son and banishment of the other, and the total ruin of her house.'[12] The only other contemporary account comes from the imperial ambassador, Chapuys:

[T]he very strange and lamentable execution of Mme. de Salisbury, the daughter of the duke of Clarence, and mother of Cardinal Pole, took place at the Tower in the presence of the Lord Mayor of London and about 150 persons more. At first, when the sentence of death was made known to her, she found the thing very strange, not knowing of what crime she was accused, nor how she had been sentenced; but at last, perceiving that there was no remedy, and that die she must, she went out of the dungeon where she was detained, and walked towards the midst of the space in front of the Tower, where there was no scaffold erected nor anything except a small block. Arrived there, after commending her soul to her Creator, she asked those present to pray for the King, the Queen, the Prince (Edward) and the Princess, to all of whom she wished to be particularly commended, and more especially to the latter, whose god-mother she had been. She sent her blessing to her, and begged also for hers. After which words she was told to make haste and place her neck on the block, which she did. But as the ordinary executor of justice was absent doing his work in the North, a wretched and blundering youth ... was chosen, who literally hacked her head and shoulders to pieces in the most pitiful manner. May God in His high grace pardon her soul, for certainly she was a most virtuous and honorable lady, and there was no need or haste to bring so ignominious a death upon her, considering that as she was then nearly ninety years old, she could not in the ordinary course of nature live long. When her death had been resolved upon, her nephew [*sic*], the son of Mr. de Montagu, who had occasionally permission to go about within the precincts of the Tower, was placed in close confinement, and it is supposed that he will soon follow his father and grandmother. May God help him![13]

The most cited account of Margaret's death, Lord Herbert of Cherbury's, is also the most dubious, being based on an unnamed source and recorded decades after the fact, and has been considerably embroidered over time. According to Lord Herbert, 'The old lady being brought to the scaffold ... was commanded to lay her head on the block; but she (as a person of great quality assured me) refused, saying, "So should traitors do, and I am none"; neither did it serve that the executioner told her, it was the fashion; so turning her gray head every way, she bid him,

"If he would have her head, to get it as he could"; so that he was constrained to fetch it off slovenly.'[14] John Lingard, writing in the nineteenth century, added the colourful, and sourceless, detail that Margaret, when ordered to lay her head on the block, responded, 'My head never committed treason; if you will have it, you must take it as you can', and had to be held down by force.[15] Neither Lord Herbert's nor Lingard's account, though, seems as likely as Chapuys's contemporary report, as there is no reason to doubt that Margaret, who had conducted herself with dignity throughout her life, behaved any differently at its end.

Margaret was buried in the Tower's chapel of St Peter ad Vincula, where Anne Boleyn had been buried in 1536 and where Katherine Howard would soon join her. On 11 November 1879, during restoration work in the chapel, a number of remains were unearthed, including those of a 'tall and aged female' supposed to be Margaret. Following an examination by F. J. Mouat, Margaret's remains were placed in a leaden coffer and respectfully reinterred.[16]

The nineteenth century was an eventful one for Margaret, who in 1886 was beatified by Pope Leo XIII as one of fifty-four English martyrs to suffer death under Henry VIII or Elizabeth, an honour she shares with Thomas More and John Fisher.[17] No one would have been more pleased by this than her son Reginald, whose first biographer, Ludovico Beccadelli, wrote that one day, upon receiving a letter written in English, Reginald announced, 'Until now I have believed that the lord God has given me the grace to be the son of one of the best and most honored ladies of England and I have gloried in that and given thanks to His Divine Majesty. But he has wished to honor me more and increase my obligation, for he has also made me a son of a martyr.'[18]

12

RESTORATION

As Chapuys feared, Margaret's death left her grandson, Henry Pole, in the Tower, with a bleak future. On 18 July 1541, Marillac wrote that his fellow prisoner, Edward Courtenay, 'is more at large than he was, and has a preceptor to teach him lessons; a thing which is not done towards the little nephew of Cardinal Pole, who is poorly and strictly kept and not desired to know anything'.[1] The lieutenant of the Tower recovered payments for his meals and those of Courtenay through 13 September 1542, after which nothing more is heard of Henry Pole.[2] There is no reason to suppose that he died of anything other than natural causes, but grief at his father's and grandmother's deaths and comparative neglect might well have hastened his death.

Following his mother's death, Reginald Pole continued to live abroad, serving the papacy in various capacities, writing and enjoying the rich intellectual life of Renaissance Italy. One of his friends was the widowed Vittoria Colonna, Marchioness of Pescara, a prominent female poet whose own friends included Michelangelo.[3] Although Vittoria was only ten years Pole's senior, after Margaret's death he asked her to 'take the place of his dead mother and to accept him as her son'. Vittoria duly addressed him as her 'son and lord' and described herself as his 'second mother'. She in turn credited Pole with curtailing her excessive fasting and other mortifications of the flesh, which had left her 'skin and bones', by advising her that she 'rather offended God than otherwise by treating her body with such austerity and rigor'. In September 1541, following Pole's appointment as papal legate to Viterbo that August, Vittoria moved to a convent there. Their constant companionship came in for some censure from other members of their religious and literary circle in Viterbo, who complained that Vittoria was too 'maternally carnal' toward Pole. It was perhaps because of this that Pole distanced himself from her somewhat, although the two corresponded regularly until Vittoria died in 1547.

Reginald's nemesis, Henry VIII, died on 28 January 1547, and was succeeded by his young son, Edward VI. In 1549, the cardinal made overtures to the Protector of England, Edward Seymour, Duke of Somerset, in the hopes of being allowed to return to England, but the effort foundered: as Mayer puts it, 'Somerset expected Pole as a private person to sue for pardon, and Pole thought it his role as a public man to advise the government on religious policy'. It did not help matters either that Somerset was a member of a gentry family raised to high status because of his sister's marriage to the king, whereas Reginald was the grandson of a duke, the son of a countess and the close kinsman of kings, and was not inclined to forget it. 'Pole dealt with Somerset as one great noble to another who badly needed to be taught manners,' Mayer comments.[4] In the event, Somerset's fall from power later in 1549 put an end to these negotiations, if they can be so termed.

Later in 1549, Pope Paul III died, leaving Pole as the favoured candidate to replace him. He needed twenty-eight votes, but could not garner more than twenty-six, which Mayer blames largely on Pole's lofty refusal to campaign.[5]

Reginald had not given up on England. In early 1553 he began working on a new edition of *De unitate*, which was to include a preface addressed to the now adolescent Edward VI, whom Reginald hoped would reverse his attainder. What Edward VI would have made of Reginald's work one can only guess, because in the spring of 1553 Edward fell ill, and on 6 July he died. One of his last acts had been to subvert the succession plan laid out by his father, who at the end of his life had provided that Mary, then Elizabeth, though both officially still illegitimate, should succeed Edward if the latter died without heirs. The fiercely Protestant Edward, however, was appalled at the devoutly Catholic Mary succeeding him, and as one might expect from Jane Seymour's son he had no doubt that Elizabeth was illegitimate. Instead, he drafted a 'Devise for the Succession' designating as heir his Protestant cousin Lady Jane Grey, granddaughter of Charles, Duke of Suffolk, and Henry VIII's sister Mary.

Mary, now thirty-seven, was having none of this. Throughout Edward's reign, as the Protestant religion was stripped literally and figuratively of Catholic trappings, Mary had fought for her right to hear Mass, and she was not going to let the wishes of a dying boy strip her of her right to rule. She had fought her battle largely unaided, for Chapuys, in failing health, had left England in 1546. Now, in what was probably her finest moment, Mary gathered troops and marched on London. Her victory was quick and bloodless. As the unfortunate Jane's councillors rushed to desert her cause, John Dudley, Duke of Northumberland, who had the task of carrying out Edward's wishes, was left essentially with the choice of fighting a losing civil war or surrendering. He surrendered, and was executed on 22 August 1553. Before that, though, Mary entered London in triumph on 3 April. Riding to the Tower, she was greeted there by a handful of kneeling prisoners, all casualties of Henry VIII's and Edward VI's reigns who hoped to win their freedom. Among them were the Duke of Norfolk, whose son had been executed near the end of Henry VIII's reign and who had barely escaped execution himself, Bishop Stephen Gardiner, imprisoned during Edward VI's reign for his resistance to religious change, and Edward Courtenay, locked up in the Tower since 1537 for his parents' role in the Exeter conspiracy. Announcing, 'Ye are my prisoners!' Mary freed them and restored them to their former positions. A month later, she made Edward Courtenay Earl of Devon.

In Italy, Reginald Pole was delighted at the news from England. 'Nothing has occurred in Christendom on which one could more reasonably congratulate any Christian mind, and especially that of your Holiness, this being a manifest victory of God over the long cogitated malice of man, corroborated by such great forces and means for the attainment of his perverse ends. And God of his goodness, to render his proceeding (operation) more illustrious, has chosen to annihilate in one moment all these long cherished projects by means of a woman,' he wrote to the Pope on 7 August. Six days later, he wrote to the new queen, congratulating and announcing his appointment as papal legate to England.[6] But Pole's return to the country he had not seen since 1532 would not be a speedy one.

Mary's reign nonetheless quickly saw the return of another Pole – Geoffrey. In the years following the death of his mother, Geoffrey had acted erratically, at one point assaulting a parson.[7] In 1548, he finally joined Reginald Pole abroad, where he remained until September 1553. Unfortunately, the new Earl of Devon, to whom Reginald Pole had written a warm letter in October 1553 congratulating upon his restoration,[8] was not well disposed to the man whom he held responsible for his father's execution. He threatened to kill Geoffrey, compelling the queen and her council to lodge him in a gentleman's house and put him under guard.[9]

Meanwhile, wrangling between the Pope, Emperor Charles and Mary's fledgling government kept Reginald Pole stalled abroad. A major sticking point was Pole's desire that lands seized from the Church be returned, which did not sit well with landowners who had turned former abbeys into country homes. Another was Mary's plans to marry Charles's son, Philip, much to the dismay of those who wanted the queen to take an English husband, with the Earl of Devon being the favoured candidate. Fears that a marriage to Philip would place England under imperial domination fuelled opposition to the marriage, and Pole was thought by the Emperor to be one of the opponents. Opposition to the match led to the uprising known as Wyatt's Rebellion, which Mary defeated in

February 1554. Among those caught up in the rebellion was the Earl of Devon, whose involvement earned him another stay in the Tower. Allowed (or pressured) to go abroad in 1555, he died in Padua on 18 September 1556 of a fever, although some suspected poisoning. His mother, Gertrude, died in 1558.[10]

From Brussels, where he was engaged in a peacemaking mission, Pole learned of Mary's defeat of Wyatt's Rebellion. He also renewed family relations with Catherine, Countess of Huntingdon, daughter of the executed Lord Montagu and sister of the young boy who had died in the Tower. Mary had restored both Catherine and her sister to their father's estates upon becoming queen,[11] and now the countess could correspond freely with her uncle, who on 21 June 1554 responded to her letter. Congratulating Catherine upon her marriage, which Pole had not known about, and praising her role as a wife and mother, he added, 'I assure you I could not read your whole letter, though it were not long, at all one time, for the sorrowful remembrance it brought me of the loss of those which I left in good state at my department, to whom you were most dearest. But when I consider ever what servants of God they were and so died, this ever doth comfort me with that certain hope of their good state in all felicity to the which we trust to one when it shall be God's pleasure to call us.'[12] Later, Pole would stand as godfather to the countess's youngest son, Walter, and would praise her eldest, Henry Hastings, for his 'gifts and graces'.[13]

Mary and Philip wed on 25 July 1554, effectively removing one obstacle to Reginald Pole's return to England. Philip then set about the process of restoring Pole to his native land and England to papal authority. At last an agreement was reached, and on 20 November 1554, Reginald arrived at Dover. Four days later, he arrived at Whitehall, where Philip and Mary (the former having been given the title of king) awaited him. Don Pedro de Cordova described the scene:

On Saturday, 24 November, Cardinal Legate Pole arrived in a barge with his cross before, and all the English lords, bishops and councillors went out in other barges to meet him. The King was dining in his chamber when he was told that the Cardinal was landing at the bridge where passengers bound for the palace step ashore, and went out to the door leading to the landing place, where the Cardinal was already standing, whom the King welcomed, bonnet in hand, with all signs of joy and courteous hospitality, and placed on his right hand. Thus they entered the palace and ascended the stairs and at the door of the first saloon found the Queen, who as soon as she saw the cross made a deep reverence to the King and Cardinal who were walking side by side. The Cardinal knelt: the Queen made him a reverence, bent down to raise him up in accordance with the custom of the country, and she and the King helped him to his feet with all the kindness to be expected on such an occasion; and there was a goodly concourse of people present.[14]

Reginald had a particular message for Mary: '*Benedictus frutus ventris tui*' – 'Blessed be the fruit of your womb'. Later, a 'Lord Montagu' – probably Geoffrey Pole – informed the cardinal that Mary was pregnant and had felt her child quicken when he greeted her.[15]
The cardinal himself made a good impression upon Don Pedro:

He is a man of most spiritual looks, and came attired in his rochet, with his hood and red cap; many there were who wept that day, so much had they longed for him, and others were sad, but did not show it. But truly that day was one of seeing and rejoicing, for it brought all that is good to England, and God showed that He had not forgotten the land, since by uniting two Catholic princes he had been pleased to reveal Himself once more to a people that had started on the road to perdition. May His name be blessed, and may He grant to the King and Queen a long life, grace to persevere, a good and Catholic Council to conduct affairs to His greater glory; may He deliver the Queen and give her a son, as it is to be hoped

He will, judging by the progress already realised through the King's prudence and tact.[16]

After greeting Mary and Philip, Reginald went to his lodgings at the Archbishop of Canterbury's residence at Lambeth; the current archbishop, Thomas Cranmer, was in prison, reaping the fruits of having helped paved the way for Henry VIII to marry Anne Boleyn.[17]

On 28 November, Pole appeared before Parliament, in the presence of Mary and Philip. So that England could once again be under the guidance of the Catholic Church, he asked those assembled to 'annul the laws and statutes against the Pope's and the Church's authority as being unreasonable and contrary to established truth'.[18] The next day, Parliament obliged, formally petitioning to be allowed back into the Catholic fold, and on the following day, St Andrew's Day, Pole returned to Parliament. There,

the Legate [Reginald] made a speech in his own tongue to the King, Queen and Parliament, praising the members and granting their petition. To the King, among other things, he said that in this first expedition he had rendered to Our Lord the great service of converting and winning back this nation to the true Catholic faith. The Emperor, he pursued, most Christian prince that he was, had long laboured to gather together materials to build the temple, which Our Lord had only permitted to be erected by his son, as befell David and Solomon. And indeed that is what happened, for so short a time has seen the completion of a mighty edifice, and one built not of perishable stuff like Solomon's, but of souls that had been led astray by evil example and doctrine. All who heard him say he spoke very eloquently; and he rose to his feet, imitated by the King and Queen, whilst the members of Parliament and all those present knelt down to receive the Legate's absolution with every sign of reverence and repentance. They then went down to chapel to hear Te Deum, and when it had been sung and the prayers said, the Legate stood in front of the altar and gave his benediction. Thus this day of St. Andrew may be counted a blessed one, and this kingdom and all other Christian realms are bound to celebrate it with fresh praise to God, Whose is the glory, and devout supplications to Him to vouchsafe His protection to England. Parliament was attended by over 500 persons, the authorised representatives of the country, who all of one accord confessed their sins and begged for mercy.[19]

John Elder wrote,

And thus England, and all we that dwell therein, account ourselves not only happy, yea and most happy, which from so many outrageous storms of errors, cares, and calamities, are thus called home again to the sure haven and port of the most holy Catholic faith but also we do believe with our very hearts, and do confess with all our mouths, that almighty God of divine providence hath preserved and kept three persons as lodestars and chief guides for the defending, in-bringing, and restoring of England thus to the unity of Christ's church.

The first is the queen's majesty, who being from her infancy a virgin, and immaculate from all spots of heresies: it hath pleased God to defend her, aide her, and save her from the hands, power, and might of her enemies, and giving her the victory over them in twinkling of an eye, which as roaring lions would have devoured her. The second is my lord cardinal, who being an exile out of his native country England, these 21 yeares ... and in the mean season so abhorred, so hated, and so detested, as no man durst scarce one name him, whom the queen's majesty now hath restored to his blood, and to the honour of his house.[20]

Margaret Pole would have heartily agreed with these sentiments.

EPILOGUE

PIOUS ENDS

Geoffrey Pole died in early November 1558, having made a 'very pious and catholic end', and was buried at Stoughton near Chichester. He had not left his family well off, as reported by Monsignor Alvise Priuli, who noted that Reginald Pole had provided for them in his will:

> Sir Geoffrey has left five sons, the eldest of whom according to the laws here will inherit that small property which scarcely sufficed to maintain in poverty the whole family, including four maiden daughters, one of whom is already with the nuns of Sion, and determined on taking the vows and living with them entirely. He also leaves two other married daughters, burdened with families, whose husbands are very poor, and these are those poor relations to whom his right reverend Lordship [Reginald Pole] desired that part of his property should be distributed. You must know that during his lifetime, both in Italy and here, the Cardinal never failed to succour them as paupers, though he never asked or received anything from the Queen either for them or for anyone else, either friend or relation, or dependent on him in any manner. Nor can I omit telling you of two examples of this nobleman's [the Cardinal's] sincerity: one is, that

being entreated very earnestly by the husband of his only sister [Henry Stafford, married to Ursula Pole] (who is also much burdened with a family, though not in such want as the brother was), merely to notify by letter to a very wealthy widow that should she wed one of these his nephews, as she seemed inclined to do, she would thereby please his right reverend Lordship, he declined to be thus persuaded by his brother-in-law, most especially because he had not a very high opinion of the young man. The other instance is this: a very wealthy gentleman having notified his intention of marrying one of his brother's daughters without any dower, but for the purpose, so far as could be seen, of being favoured and assisted by the Cardinal in a very important lawsuit, his right reverend Lordship gave him to understand that in his suit he could have justice and nothing else; so the intended marriage was broken off.[1]

Geoffrey's oldest son, Arthur, and another son, Edmund, imprudently pressed Arthur's claim to the throne, then that of Mary, Queen of Scots, during Elizabeth's reign and ended up in the Tower, where they died sometime before 1570, having commemorated their stay with inscriptions in the Salt Tower and the Beauchamp Tower. Constance Pole, Geoffrey's widow, made her will on 12 August 1570 and died soon thereafter, having asked to be buried next to her 'dear and well-beloved husband'.[2]

Ursula Pole, married to Henry Stafford, was fortunate in having a husband who after his own father's execution had assiduously avoided controversy, devoting himself instead to his family archives and his impressive library. The couple and their large family fared well during Mary's reign, receiving the Stafford ancestral estate of Thornbury. Ursula died in 1570, seven years after her husband. She was the last of Margaret's children to die.[3]

The optimism surrounding Mary's reign in 1554 was unfounded. Mary's longed-for pregnancy proved to be illusory; in a cruel twist of fate, Mary had yet another phantom pregnancy in 1557–58. Philip, whose priorities lay with the Empire, soon left England, returning only briefly. The Marian persecutions, resulting in over 300 men and women being burned alive, demoralized the country and left a pall on Mary's reputation, overshadowing her achievements, not the least of which was her paving the way for her younger sister to rule.

One of the first to die at the stake was Thomas Cranmer, who was martyred on 20 March 1556. He had already been succeeded by Reginald Pole, who became Archbishop of Canterbury on 11 December 1555. Reginald would hold the position for less than three years.[4]

By the spring of 1558, Mary's health was failing, and in August, she made a codicil to her will. Under pressure to provide for the succession, the childless queen reluctantly accepted her younger sister as her heir. On 16 November, having heard Mass at six in the morning, she died before seven in the morning, aged forty-two.

When Mary died, few mourned; all eyes were turned to Anne Boleyn's daughter. Philip, across the sea from his queen, expressed only polite regret at her demise. The man who might have stood at Mary's side during her last hours was unable to do so, because at fifty-eight he too was on his deathbed. Upon hearing of the queen's death,

> after remaining silent for a short while, he then said ... that in the whole course of his life nothing had ever yielded him greater pleasure and contentment than the contemplation of God's providence as displayed in his own person and in that of others, and that in the course of the Queen's life, and of his own, he had ever remarked a great conformity, as she, like himself, had been harassed during many years for one and the same cause, and afterwards, when it pleased God to raise her to the throne, he had greatly participated in all her other troubles entailed by that elevation.

Twelve hours after Margaret Pole's charge Mary died, Margaret's son died 'so placidly that he seemed to sleep rather than to die, as did the Queen likewise, so that had not a physician perceived the act her Majesty would have died without any one's witnessing it'.[5] Reginald's 'great conformity' had held true to the end.

APPENDIX 1

THE EVIDENCE IN THE EXETER CONSPIRACY: A SELECTION

Below is a selection of statements made by Margaret, her sons, and several others who were questioned in the so-called Exeter Conspiracy. These statements and those by other witnesses are calendared in *Letters and Papers, Foreign and Domestic, Henry VIII, Volume 13 Part 2, August–December 1538*. Footnotes and their accompanying references have been removed; otherwise, the statements include the editorial emendations as they appear in the original source. Spelling has not been altered.

Statements of Margaret Pole
Answer of the countess of Salisbury to certain interrogatories ministered to her by my lord Admiral and the bp. of Ely, 12 & 13 Nov. 30 Henry VIII.

1. Being asked whether cardinal Pools, before his going beyond seas, opened his mind to her, saying he liked not the proceedings of this realm and for that reason would go beyond sea, and left her these words for a token, *spes mea*, &c.; she replies that he never opened his mind to her touching any statutes or proceedings of the King and it was sore against her mind that ever he went abroad "again." And that she takes the King to

witness, for she desired his Grace that her son might no more go over sea; neither was there any privy token between her and him at his departure; but the words *spes mea*, &c, is a common word written in the windows and other places of the house. She knew none other but that the King had sent him to Paris upon his business.

2. Examined whether the vicar of Est Maigne at his departure opened his mind to her after like sort; replies that he never did about his going beyond sea, but brought home her children and said that within a sevennight or a fortnight he would return again, [as she] supposed "he would have done ... made her privy of anything what he ... ne. axed her for token, letter or message [unto her] son."

3. Examined whether [at any ti]me she received any letters or messages from [the sai]d Poole by Th[r]ogmerton, "and that she and her ... should hold up yea and nay and speak little ":— Denies utterly that she ever received any letters or message by Throgmerton or any other concerning Reginald Poole except one from the King, of which she has a copy.

4. As to the sending over of Hugh Holland, says it was not by her consent or with her knowledge.

5. Asked whether Sir Geoffrey Poole ever told her that the King went about to cause Sir Reynold Poole to be slain; says he did, and she prayed God heartily to change the King's mind. And being examined who told her that the Cardinal had escaped that danger, she says both her sons; and for motherly pity she could not but rejoice.

6. Asked whether she [knew] that Peter Meotas was gone over the sea [for] killing her son, and that both her sons would go to the Cardinal. Denies that she ever heard that Peter Meotas should so do, and prays God she may be torn in pieces if ever she heard such a thing of her sons.

7. Asked whether the Cardinal desired her blessing and thought she would [be glad of his blessing again, putting her in remembrance of the communication had at his departing, and

th[at s]he and her sons should hold up yea and [nay] and that they should tarry in England still, &c. Replies that she never heard any such thing, either by word of mouth or letters.

8. Examined whether in their communications all three together they have much commended the doings of the Cardinal, trusting he should be Pope one day and come into England again:—Denies that they ever had such conversation, but has often wished to see him again in England with the King's favour, though he were but a poor parish priest.

9. Examined of certain communications they had together, wherein they lamented the King's proceedings and wished for a change : she utterly denies it. "And where it was objected that she liked not the plucking d[own] of the abbeys and houses of religion [she] saith [true] it was she was sorry for ... of the houses where her ancestors lay [though she] much lamented the living of the ... which was the cause of th ... thereof."

10. As to the [going o]ver of Morgan she utterly denies that she heard thereof. Also denies she ever heard lord Montacute say that none ruled about the King but knaves.

11. Examined whether when they heard that Hugh Holland was taken, all three by one consent burned their letters, whether received from Sir Reynold Poole or my lord of Exeter and his wife:—Replies that she herself never burned any letter concerning the King. Has burned private men's letters of small importance, but there never was such agreement among them and she never heard of any that her sons had burned. Denies she ever received letters or messages from my lord of Exeter or his wife prejudicial to the King or his realm. Denies also that she ever heard her son say that this world was turned upside down, or that it would come to stripes, or that she ever heard her son wish or look for the King's death or "mention any stirring or motion or thing like days of her life."

12. Asked whether she heard the lord Montacate say [he h]ad rather dwell in the West parts [than] at Warblington, and that he lamented the death of lord Aburgeyveny because he was

able to make 10,000 men; says she never heard such things. nor that she heard him say that my lord marquis of Exeter was his ass[ured] friend and 'would take such party [as] he took.

13. Examined of the lord Montacute's saying. "beshrewing the lord Darcy because he left so soon at the last insurrection, and saying he played the fool going about to pluck away the [Cou]ns[el] for he should have gone abouts to pluck away the head":—Answers "upon her damnation," she never heard such words spoken.

14. "Item, [examin]ed of the lord Montacute h[is] saying [be]cause the King came not to Warblington, We shall thank them one day, and a time will come, &c." Never heard her son say so, and thinks him very much belied. Denies also that ever there was any agreement to conceal anything among them.

15. Says also she [never heard] any little inkling of any such decei[t as] our master should have been deceived by [the] French king; but says her son Sir Geoffrey being in an Inn of Court, went over sea to the interview at Guisnes without her knowledge or that of lord Montacute till he came thither, and if lord Montacute had not made him return he would have gone in w[arf]ayre (:).

16. Being examined further u[nder] whom; says she knows not.

17. As to the article that lord Montague and Sir Geoffrey should wish themselves to be over seas sometime with their brother, sometime with the bp. of Luke. "she denieth utterly her baptism and prayeth that she never see God in the face if ever she heard any such words" As to the last article, "that this world must needs change and come to stripes, and at that time th[eir] being in England should be occasion of m[o]re favour to be showed to others within this realm, with great oaths swearing she saith she never heard no such words."

18. Examined of Hierome and Nanfant; says they came upon Saturday both to her house, and Nanfant went away upon Sunday, and Hierome on Monday, and the cause of their coming was for the … and the tone for seeing his wie[f, and

s]he commanded them to depart, for [she woul]d not suffer them tarry; and Jerome [we]nt into Buckinghamshire to my lord Montacute's house : and as for the other she cannot tell whither." Signed.

19. "Item she [said] that communing of her son Geoffrey with the Con[tro]ller of her house he said to her; Take heed of h[im], Madame, for I fear me. Madame, one da[y he] will do you a displeasure,' 'Why, what [displeasure?' saith she. 'Peradventure,' said h[e, 's]lyppe away.' 'Nay.' Nay' said she. he will not be so unhappy.'

  "Item, she said, when she spake with the King his Grace he showed her how her son had written against him. Alas ... thy what grief is this to me to see him whom ... set up to be so ungracious and unhappy. And up[on th]is when her son Montague came home to her ... she said to him, 'What hath the King shown me of [my] son? Alas, son, said she, what a child have I [in] him!' And then my lord Montague consay[led he]r to declare him us a traitor to their servan[ts], that they might so report him when they came in to their countries. And so she called her servants and declared unto them accordingly. She took her said son for a traitor and for no son, and that she would never take him otherwise." Signed.

20. Protestation that all she has said is true. Signed.

21. "At Cowdrey:—Item, she being exami[ned touchin]g the copy of the letter found in her gentilw[oman's chest] saith and confesseth that her steward wrote [the sa]me letter to my lord Montacute by her consent, [bu]t not since he was in the Tower, but she cau[se]d it to be written since Sir Geoffrey was taken." Signed.

Pp. 8. Mutilated and illegible. Each page signed at the bottom Margaret (or Margret) Salysbery, and sometimes separate articles are so signed, but the greater part of the signature is in most cases lost.

[item 818]

Statements and Correspondence of Geoffrey Pole
Examination of Sir Geoffrey Pole.

He confesses that he liked well the doings of his brother the
Cardinal and misliked the proceedings in this realm. That he
and many others with whom he has conferred have wished a
change of this world without meaning any hurt to the King. Being
asked with whom he had so conferred he replied the [lord De la
Warr], Mr. Croftes, resident in Chichester, Freende and Langley,
prebendaries of the same church. Also that the lord De la Warr
about 12 months [ago] was of that opinion, but of late when
the King was in Sussex he declared himself to be indifferent, in
such conferences as this examinate had with him. Also the lord
Montacute his brother was of the same opinion before the death
of his wife, but since that time he has found him more indifferent.
Also the marquis of Exeter was at first of the same mind, but
he has not spoken with him for nearly two years; but by his
communications with lord Montacute during these two years he
knows that the Marquis and his said brother were of one opinion.
Further, he heard Sir Edward Nevill say he trusted this world would
amend one day. Also the bp. of London said in conversation with
this examinate "that he was but a syfer, for [the] lord Privy Seal
first, and [then the] bishop of [Roch]ester, have appointed heretics
to preach at Paul's Cr[oss]. And further he sayeth that within
a twelvemonths he hath heard Mrs. Roper and Mrs. Clement
s[ay th]at they liked not this plucking down of abbeys, im[ages
an]d pilgrimages, and prayed God to send a change. [An]d after
being examined what he meant by [the] word indifferent, which,
in his examination before, touched the lord De la Warr and the
lord Montacute, answereth he meant that they were not so much
affectionate to that part as they were at the former conferences."
Being asked what change was wished for; he replies that they
wished this world of plucking down abbeys and pilgrimages, and
this manner of preaching to be changed, but not the King's person.
Finally, examinate besought the King "that he may have good
keeping and cherishing and thereby somewhat comfort himself

and have better stay of himself," and he would then fully open all that he knew, whomsoever it might touch, whether mother, brother, uncle, or any other. Being further examined whether he had intended to have gone over sea to his brother, he says he did not intend to go to his brother, but to Louvain to speak with the vicar of Est Mayn.

"This examination was knowledged written and after openly read and knowledged again the 26th day of October anno 30 Regis Henrici Octavi in the presence of us." Signed: W. Southampton— per me Edmundum Walsyngham—Rich. Crumwell—per me Nicholaum Heyth—William Peter.

[item 695]

A very mutilated letter, probably seized at the time of Sir Geoffrey Pole's arrest.

"I have wretten to you ofter then I per [adventure ... to] have don and not so ofte n dede a[s] ... I have used was for the nonce ... not off no slugyshnes ... here that you receved eny on ... wherin I ... a letter r ... sylence [a]nd ... you ... ... because you lake the comodety ... so ofte as you wold then that you ... .or that I shold lyghtly p ... our frendshyp is knytt fast nere to ... .shold set our minds far fro othe [r] ... habes et semper habebis. I am g ... ther to your cheff desyre that is ... helthe to encrece long ther in ... hertes desyre and God's pleasure ... vale ex animo. Lordyngtoni p ...

In Sir Geoffrey Pole's hand.

[item 696]

Original record of the second examination of Sir Geoffrey Pole.

At the end, in Pole's own hand: "Sir, I beseech your noble Grace to pardon my wretchedness that I have not done my bounden duty unto your Grace heretofore as I have ought to have done, but Sir, grace coming to me to consider your nobleness always to me, and now especially in my extreme necessity, as I perceive by my lord Admiral and Mr. Controller, your goodness shall not be lost on me, but surely as I found your Grace always faithful unto me, so

I refuse all creature living to be faithful to you. Your humble slave, Geffrey Pole."

[item 743]

Sir Geoffrey Pole's Statement.

"And fyrst ... Devell f ... fall off h ... kyng off ... Arthur ... c ... off . arance ... put a innocent to dethe.

"Item, he sayd that the King's Grace ... that h[e wou]ld gyve all England ... kepyng the trew y ... the lord Monta[gue] ... promyse worshipfully ... xx ... he forsoke hys wyff and made hys i[ssue that h] e had by her bastard [and] so yn h[er ly]ff tyme the Kyng marryd a harlot [and] a heretyke [and] kyllyd his good wyff with unkindness."

Item, he sayd he helped his brother Reynold to depart the realm that he might not aid the King's purpose in forsaking his wife.

"Item, he sayd that all princes cristen hathe the Kyng yn mockage for so handelyng the mattar that when he had spent great somis off money [and] saw trowth ayenst ... cyon off the chyrc[h w]hyche ... he have done with losse cost ... well worthy off more ... e so nawghty a woman ... kyng but was the ... body [and] the disci ... man [and] fynall ... ... reall ... subvertyng [G]ods law [and] [m]ans law contrary to all ryght and [e]quyte.

"[Item, he s]ayd it was not mattar of concyence b ... he love to forsake ... ew wyff [and] to ... ne to forsake a ... [and] ta ... heretyk.

"Item, he sayd it w ... ot . r ... ryly ... to tro . the to extynct the po[pe's powe]re but [wilfu]llnes to have ill lyberty to do [what] hym lyst.

"Item, he sayd that afor th[e Ky]ngs my[nd] was set upon devorse off the good quene [and] not [ca]tched yn the snare off unlawfull love with the lady Ane, the Kyng cowld byd well ynowghe the auctoryte off the Pope thowgh he myslykyd hys abuses.

"Item, he seyd because the Pope wold not grawnt to the incestuose mariage the Kyng forsoke hys auctority with all hys good uses [and] abuses.

"Item, he sayd that al wyse vertuos[e] [and] [g]ood men [and] faythfull ware ayenst the [King's] purposes [both] off hys unlawfull mariage [and] al[so the] forsaky[ng] off the auctoryte off the Pope.

"Item, he sayd that knaves and heretycks and smatterers off lerny[ng] ware the Kyngs assisters in bothe thes unlawfull enterprises.

"Item, he seyd the [sam]e knaves [de]vyse [by l]aw to kyll [and] slaye as m[any] as wol ... [a]yen saye the Kyngs [pur]pose ... yg . hat ... hat they cowld [nei]ther by reason nor equyte.

"Item, he sayd that comen knowen kn[aves g]even to all mysheff, settyng at nowght bothe Go[d and D]evyll, open rybawlds, [w]ar avanced [and] good m[en and ver]tuose m[en] ... choppyng off hedds.

"Item, [he sayd th]e Turke was more ch ... h ... su ... [t]hen the Kyng beyng a cristen prince.

"Item, h[e sa]yd that the Kyng and Cromwell ware bo[the] off on nature, [and] what becam of the nobyltye off the hole realme they cared not so they might lyve themselffs at ther owne pleasor.

"Item, he seyd that thoughe the Kyng gloryed with the tytylle to be Supreme Hede next God, yet he had a sore lege that no pore man wold be glad off, and that he shold not lyve long for all his auctoryte next God.

"Item, he shewed me at Bockmar that he dremyd the Kyng was dede. "And now," quoth he, "we shall see some rufflyng [and] byd Mr. Cromwell good deane with all hys devyses."

"Item, he say[d thou]ghe we have a prince yet th ... begyld for the Kyng [and] hys [whole i]ssue s[tan]d accursyd.

"Item, he sayd when ... was taken and all thyn[gs] peasyd, thowghe the Kyng thow[ght him]selff then sewre yet ther wold come, anoth[er] ... that wold p ... [and] ... yse cownsellors (?).

"Item, ... had ... manly sto ... they were now ... [confo]rmable to hys wyll ... d on day leve the [realm] alone [and] lyve beyond the seas, saying wher be y[ou then?].

"[Item, he sayd] that hym selff thowg[ht] that all the R[ealm] ... well apayd to be o ... a ...

"I[tem, he sayd t]he Kyngs Grace told h ... of Scotts whyche kyllyd not only ... [p]oysonyd the quene of Scotts but also all her ... blod that war not gylte therin. And so, 'quod he,' 'the Kyng to be revengyd off Reynold, I fere, wyll kyll us all.'

"Item, hewyshed hym selffand me with the byshopp off Luke, for he was a ryght honest man [and] a great frend of Reynolds. 'Mary,' quod I, 'and vow fere syche jeopardy, lett us be walkyng hens quyckly.'

"Item, he sayd that yet we shold do more, and here whe[n] the tyme sholde come, what wt powre and frendship, nor it is not the pluckyng downe off thes knaves that wyll help the mattar; we must pluk downe the hede, and that I was but a fole to thynke otherwyse; but for all hys wysdom [I] beshrew hys hed (?) for hys so meanyng and so saying."

[item 800]

The second examination of the said Sir Geoffrey Pole, taken 2 Nov. anno predicto.

All he said at his former examination is true, and he "knowledgeth the examination, being at this time wholly read unto him, to be true in every part thereof." When his brother the Cardinal was at an abbey beside Cambray, Hugh Holland, then retaining to him, asked him if he would anything to his said brother. Replied he would write nothing. "No marry!" said Hugh "Nor I will carry no letters." Said then, "Commend me unto him, and show him what you hear here, and how the rumour is that he shall be slain." Hugh reported on his return that the Cardinal had said he marvelled that the King, when he could not be revenged on him himself, "went about to set others, as the French king, upon him, and that the French king had sent him letters which the King had sent him for that purpose." The Cardinal had said if mother, brother, or any oth[er of his] kin were of the same opinion as the King and others of this realm, he would tread upon them with his feet. Knows of no letters or money being sent to the Cardinal by his mother, brother, or any other. Examined who first showed him the King [intende]d anything against the Cardinal; "Mrs. Da[rrell showed] him thereof" and afterwards lord Montacute at his own house told him the same Sent word by Hugh Holland that he would come over sea if the Cardinal desired it; but got the reply "that both he and the lord Montacute [his] brother should tarry in England and hold up yea and nay the[re, for] he would do well enough." Hugh reported that the Cardinal asked about the bishops in England and prayed God amend them.

Doctor Sterkey "showed him that he had written certain letters and after spoken with Mr. Wriothesley, and that in communication Mr. Wriothesley said that this examinate and other of his family must not be made co[kneyes], and after the said Sterkey said further that the lord Pr[ivy] Seall, if the King war nott of a good nature, for one Pole's [sake] would destroy all Poles," and "that the bishops of Durham and Chichester read [togethers] the cardinal Pole's book."

Third examination of the same, taken 3 Nov.

Hugh Holland further reported that the Cardinal desired to be commended to lord Montacute and examinate, and hoped to come to England himself, and bade him remind lord Montacute of their communication at the Cardinal's departure. Throckmerton also desired Hugh to remind lord Montacute of their communication at his last being in England, and say that when he would come over sea Throckmorton would come himself and fetch him. When examinate waited at Court lord Montacute regarded him little, and said they were flatterers that followed the Court and none served the King but knaves. After he was forbidden the Court lord Montacute regarded him more and showed him copies of two letters which he thinks Throckmerton brought, one to the King and one to the lord Privy Seal. Once, in examinate's house, lord Montacute wished they were both over sea with the bp. of Luke, for this world would one day come to stripes, and then their being here might be "occasion of more favour to be showed in the realm." After Mrs. Darell showed him of the displeasure intended to the Cardinal he went to lord Montacute's house and found him in his garden. Said, "I hear that our brother beyond the sea shall be slain." "No," said lord Montacute," "he is escaped, I have letters." Thinks these letters were either from Mrs. Darell or the lady Marquis of Exeter. Saw letters from the lady Marquis to lord Montacute "wherein was contained that communication be[ing in the] Council [o]f the lord Montacute, the lord Marquis her [husband] offered himself to be bound body for body for him."

Asked Dr. Sterkey "whow [the bishops] of Duresrae and Chichester" liked the book written by the Cardinal when they read it. He replied that they said the matter of the book "was very clerkly handled, and that it could not be better handled, saving it was written very ve[hement]ly." Showed lord Montacute all that Hugh reported from the Cardinal, but did not tell who was the messenger.

Fourth examination taken 5 November.

Examined where and when he opened to lord Montacute the message sent by Hugh Holland, says it was a little before the King's coming to Sussex last summer, in riding between lord De Laware's house and Warbyngton. Examined of the conferences between him and Croftes of Chichester; told Croftes all the message from the Cardinal. Croftes said, "Well it is he (the Cardinal) that shall restore the Church again." Croftes said the lord Privy Seal "promised the lords at the arraignment of lord Darcy, that if they would cast him he should neither lose life, nor goods." Because the King, when at Stansted, came not to my Lady their mother, lord Montacute said, "Well, [le]t it pass, we shall thank them one day. This world will turn up so down, and I fear me we shall have no lack b[ut] of honest men." Lord Monacute told examinate, at the raffle when Holland was taken, that he had burned many letters at his house called Bukmar, beside Henley upon Temmes. Lord Montacute showed him within an arrow shot of Hounsloe the letters from my lady marquis of Exeter: they were all in her own hand. The lord Montacute showed him this summer that the lord Privy Seal had sent Mr. Richard

Crumwell to the marquis of Exeter "to be frank in opening certain things"; but the lord Marquis replied he would open nothing to the hindrance of his friend; another time the lord Privy Seal had sent to the lord Marquis to his house in London "concerning a certain berwarde." Asked lord Montacute the cause of a certain strangeness he had noticed of late between lord Montacute and the Marquis; Montacute said, "Marry ! My lord Marquis hath willed so, because there is noted a certain suspicion between us." There were frequent letters between the lady Marquis and lord Montacute.

Fifth examination, taken 7 Nov.

Lord Montacute, in conversation with him, often wished they were over sea with the bp. of Luke; he did so at Chiphames, "in a certain morn [ing since the] departing of his brother, the Cardinal, from Flanders." Was not trusted by the lady Marquis after it was perceived the King favoured him; the lord [Montacute] told him this. "The lord Marquis, a certain time at Hors[ley], at which time he gave the lord Privy Seal a summer coat and a wood knife, winking upon this examinate, said, 'Peace! knaves rule about the King'; and holding [up] and shaking his fist, said, 'I trust to give them a buffet one day.'" Lord Montacute used to say a time would come, and he feared they would lack nothing but honest men. Once met the lord Marquis riding from London to his house at Horsley and examinate's servant came at the same time with letters from London. Turned back with the lord Marquis, who said he had been compelled to leave his constableship of Windsor and take abbey lands instead. "What !" said examinate, "be you come to this point to take abbey lands now?" "Yea," said he, "good enough for a time; they must have all again one day." Once asked lord Montacute why he had no more mind to Warbyngton, and he replied," I would rather dwell in the West parts, my lord marquis of Exeter is strong there, and I am sorry the lord Aburgavenney is dead, for if he were alive he were able to make 10,000 men." Lord Montague said that when the lord Marquis was put out of the Privy Chamber, the putting out of others at the same time was only done to colour the putting out of the lord Marquis. One Colens, a [priest], belonging to the lord Montacute, showed examinate that one Morgan, servant also of lord Montacute, was to have gone over sea to kill Peter Meotes or whoever should kill cardinal Pole. Mrs. Darell said that one of the French king's Privy Chamber, very friendly with Sir Francis Bryan, warned the Cardinal that they intended to slay him. When examinate was banished the Court lord Montacute said to him, "Geoffrey, God loveth us well that will not suffer us to be amongst them; for none rule about the Court but knaves." At that time "lying in bed with his said brother," the latter said "I dreamed now that the King is dead." Two days after he said in his great chamber at Bockmar, "The King is not dead, but he will one day die suddenly; his leg will kill him and then we shall have jol[ly] stirring." After last insurrection lord Montacute said in his own ground at Luftington, "Twishe ! Geoffrey, thou hast no cast with [thee; the lord] Darcye played the fool; he went about to p[luck away the] Council. He should first have begun with [the head; but I beshrew] them for leaving off so soon."

Sixth examination, taken 9 and 11 Nov.

When the [King] and the French king last met beyond sea, examinate was there in disguise and present at the meeting, but never went abroad except at night, keeping all day in the chamber of his brother the lord Montacute, who said he thought the French king would deceive the King. Since then lord Montacute was never pleased with the King's doings. The lord marquis of Exeter knew that examinate was then in Calais. Lord Montacute told him last summer, riding between Halfnakyd and Chichester never to open anything if he should be examined, for if he opened one all must needs come out. Says also he was told by his wife that lord Montacute asked her how he (examinate) did since his coming to the Tower adding that he had heard that he was mad [and that it] "forceth not what a mad man saith." Also that at the [King's] being beyond the seas of which he spake before, t[he lord Mon]tacute sent this examinate to the princess Dowager to [tell] her that nothing was done at that meeting touching the marriage with the lady Anne, and that the King had done his best but the French king would not assent to it. Also that the earl of Huntingdon and lord Montacute at divers Parliaments, communing together, "would say they [were but] knaves and heretics that gave over, and that such as did [agree to] things there did the same for fear, an I did always murmur and grudge against things determined there. He saith also that at the last insurrection the lord Montacute promised this examinate harness for himself and 10 more," Montacute being then at Bisham. Examinate asked him afterwards where the harness was. He replied, In a corner, "but that forced not; he knew it should not need at that time." He has heard Montacute say that Reynold (meaning the Cardinal his brother) should do good one day. Says also that Hierome Raglande had been very familiar with Montacute, and known much of his mind. That Thos. Nanfant also knew much, and was wont to go often in errands (?) for him to the lord Marquis and others, and that Montacute put the said Nanfant to Sir John Wallop in France to learn the French tongue. Also at his coming from Calais, of which he spake before, he came by the lady Salisbury his mother, then in Kent, and brought letters to her from lord Montacute her son. Also that Montacute lately lamented very much the sickness of the lady Marquis, "saying that his stomach was such that if the wisdom of my Lady were not, he would not be able to bear this world, and feared nothing [in the lord] Marquis but that he would die before the time sh[ould come]." Says also that when at Calais he heard [the lord Monta]cute say that the French king "was hardier ma[n] th[an the] King our master" and that when one Kend[al] and others were in the Tower he heard lord Montacute say that it was pity the lord Marquis was so handled, and that he had a just suit depending in the law for that matter.

The seventh examination of the said Sir Geoffrey, taken 12 Nov.

Says he has heard Sir Edward Nevell many times deprave the King, saying that his Highness was a beast and worse than a beast. Also that lord Montacute was never willing that this examinate should serve the King, but was content that he should sa[rve t]he lady Dowager. The lord Monacute also advised this examinate not to go from his mistress, and after, when this examinate asked him to help him into the King's service, he would not but he would have the marquis of Exeter's advice therein. Getting no comfort of them, made suit himself to the King, when the King accepted him, at which lord Montacute was not content. Lord Montacute told him also the King would go so far that all the world would mislike him, and that the King one day told the lords "that he [would] go from them one day, and where be you then?" and the lord Montacute said, "If he will serve us so, we shall be happily rid." Lord Montacute has confessed to him that he never loved the King from childhood, and that King Henry VII had no affection nor fancy unto him. He said also "that the King would be out of his wits [on]e day, for when he came to his chamber he would look angerly, and after fall to fighting." He says also that he told Croftes of Chichester of Hugh Holland's going to cardinal Pole, and Croftes advised him to go over with him, saying it was that cardinal that should do good one day, and gave examinate 20 nobles towards his charges, saying "You may be able to do good another day." Two days after Croftes wrote to him that he had a vision in the night that he should do better here than if he went over sea, and examinate paid him the 20 nobles back. He says also that last summer lord Montacute and this examinate rode together to lord Stafford's h[ouse], when lord Stafford showed him he was afraid to converse with lord Montacute. "I like him not; he dare speak so largely." Lord Stafford told him also, "Ye foll[ow] so much the lord Montacute that [he will b]e your undoing one day." He says also that at the King's last [be]ing in Cowdrey, Sir Edw. Nevell said to this examinate, "[Master] Pole, let us not be seen to speak togethers; we be had in suspicion; but it forceth not, we shall do well enough one day." Sir Edw. Nevell another time told him at the Court, when the King was at Westminster, "God's blood ! I am made a fool amongst them, but I laugh [and] make merry to drive forth the time. The King keepeth a sort [of] knaves here that we dare nother look nor speak, and [if I were] able to live, I would rather live any life in the wo[rld than] tarry in the Privy Chamber."

[item 804]

Notes from depositions.

"Geoffray Pole:—"Item, ... the Kyng was a ... the Kyngz palays at Westm. an ... Sir Edwarde wolde saye th ... sytte slepyng, ye and soma t[imes ... slepe etyng lyke a beeste.

"Item, the seide Sir Edwa[rde] ... Sir Geoffray, Be mery ... chaunge oone daye. And th ... we shall have a daye upo[n] ... these words hathe he spoken u ... of Westminster, and also diverse tym[es] ... waye within these twoo yeres."

[item 830]

Articles against the prisoners, taken from their own confessions, with marginal references to folios in some book of depositions:—

Headed: To be given in evidence.

"Sir Geoffrey Pole sayeth that Croftes hath declared to him that they did like well the proceedings of the card. Pole and misliked the proceedings of this realm and wished for a change of this world." Signed: Geffrey Pole.

Sir Geoffrey showed Croftes of Hugh Holland's going to the Cardinal, and Croftes exhorted Sir Geoffrey to go over sea, "saying that it was the Cardinal that should do good [one] day, and gave Sir Geoffrey 20 nobles towards his charges, saying, 'Go. Ye may be able to do good another day.'" And within two days after Croftes wrote to Geoffrey that he had a vycyon in t[he n]yght from Our Lady that he should do better here than if he went over sea; and thereupon Sir Geoffrey paid the 20 nobles again." Signed by Sir Geoffrey.

Geoffrey Pole['s confession].

1. He says "that ... Nevill of these things he he[rd Sir Edward Nevyll] say [that] he trusted the world would amend one day." He has heard Sir Edw. Nevill at Westminster most abominably deprave the King, saying that he was a beast and worse than a beast. That at [the King's] last being at Cowdrey, Sir Edw. Nevill said "Cousin, [let] us not be seen to speak togethers, for we be had in [suspicion; ye] t it forceth not, we shall do well enough one day."4. That Sir Edw. Nevill showed him " ... God's blood, I am made a fool among them, but I laugh and make merry to drive forth the time. The King keepeth a court of knaves here that we [dare no]ther loke nor speak, and I were able to live I wolde rather [live any] lyfe in the world then tary in the pryvye Chamber." Each of these articles signed by Sir Geoffrey Pole. Sir Geoffrey Pole says that Hugh Holland showed him that card. Pole told him beyond sea "that if his own brother or any other of his kin were of that opinion, that the King and other of his realm be of, that he would defye [the]ym and tread upon the[ym] with his feate." Signed: Gefferey Pole.

[item 830]

Depositions of Sir Geoffrey Pole touching the lady Marquis.
After Mrs. Darell showed him of the intended displeasure against his brother the Cardinal, he went to lord Montacute in his garden and said "Marry, I hear that our brother beyond the sea shall be slain." "No," said Montacute, "he is escaped. I have letters." Thinks the letters were either from Mrs. Darell or from the lady Marquis of Exeter. Saw letters of the lady Marquis to lord Montacute containing that when the latter was spoken of in the Council the lord Marquis had offered to be bound for him. Montacute showed him the letters beside Hounslow: they were all in the lady Marquis' hand. The lady Marquis once bore him good mind; "but after it was perceived that the King favour[ed] this

examinate they said he would tell all and therefore trusted him no le[nger]."

[item 831]

Depositions touching the lord Delaware.
    Of Sir Geoffrey Poole.
    Examined with whom he has spoken who misliked the proceedings in the realm and wished for a change: Says lord Delaware, twelve months ago, was of that opinion, but lately, when the King was in Sussex, Delaware said he was not so inclined to that as he had been.

[item 831]

Statements of Henry Pole, Lord Montagu
His examination, 7 Nov. 30 Hen. VIII.
    "The lord Montacute confesseth" he received letters from the lady Marquis, saying her husband had offered "in counsayle" to be bound "body for body" for him. The lord Marquis in his own house showed examinate that the lord Privy Seal had sent to know who showed him of his servant that then was in prison, and he had answered he would never disclose his friend if it touched not the King. At the King's late being at the lord Marquis' house, the lord Marquis told him (examinate?) he had been warned by friends to avoid his company. "He saith also that he hath lived in prison all these six years." Doctor Sterkey told him his brother the Cardinal, then in Flanders, should be brought home quick or dead, "and that Peter Meotes [was gone over sea], and would rid him one way or other." Related this "to [Elizabeth Dar]ell." "His brother Sir [Geoffrey in communica]tion showed him that the keeping of letters m[ight turn a manne]s friend to hurt, and this examinate answered again, Nay they shall hurt no fry[nde] of mine for I have bur[ned all] my letters. He sayeth also upon further examination [that he hath been pre]sent when Sir Edward Nevell hath song [merry songs. And] the lady Marq[uis bein]g also present ha[th willed] hym to st[o]p or s[tay] ther, [but] he

sayeth that he never heard Sir Edward Nevell utter a[nything] in those songs other than merry things. He sayeth also that [he was at Hackney] on Sunday last, and there spake with [Mres.] D[a]rell; [Examy]nyd [for whatt] cause he w[ent thither, and] of whatt [things he] then [and there com]munyd [with her. awnswereth that Sir Anthonie Hungerforde] being of late in the town, and communication being begun between this examinate, the said Sir Anthony and Mres Darrell" touching 100*l*. due to Mrs. Darrell, he then went to show Mrs. Darrell that Sir Anthony was gone from London, and no good could be done therein. Mrs. Darrell showed him "that his brother Sir Geoffrey had almost slain himself, and lamented that act." Has often said he liked not Warblinton, and that he would to God the lord Aburgavenney "had not died, for his son's sake." Signed: Henry Mount[agu].

[item 772]

Depositions of lord Montacute touching the lady Marquis.

Received letters from my lady Marquis saying that her husband had offered in Council to be bound body for body for him. Has heard Sir Edward Nevell sing merry songs when the lady Marquis was present "and willed him to stop or stay there."

[item 831]

Statements of Constance Pole (wife of Geoffrey Pole)
Examination of Dame Constance, wife of Sir Geoff. Pole, 11 Nov. Says that between [Whi]tsuntide andM[idsummer] last she received a [ring] for a token by Colyns, a priest belonging to lord [Mont]acute. whom, upon that token, she brought to her husband's closet where he burned five or six letters the contents of which she knows not. Colyns at the same time told her that her husband would [be] at Luftington the day following; but he was not, for both he and lord Montacute [went] together to London. She says also that since her husband's imprisonment, speaking with lord Montacute of how it was said he was in a frenzy and might utter rash things, he remarked, "It forceth not what a madman [speaketh]." Says also that at such times

as lord Montacute came to Luftington he was accustomed to walk abroad, in ch[urch]es and other places adjoining, with her husband, but of their communications she knoweth nothing. She says also she has heard lord Montacute say he liked not the air of Warblington; also that lord Montacute and her husband "lying one time [at] night at Luftington, they both rode together on the m[orn]ing to a place called Raughey besides Horsham, in Sussex, where at that time lay the lord Stafford," but to what intent she knows not.

[item 796]

Statements of Gertrude Courtenay, Marchioness of Exeter
6 Nov:—"The lady Marques" examined, confesses that she showed lord Montacute that her husband was admonished by some friends to keep no company with him; she also told him the King had sent to her husband in his house in London for a certain bearward; and that she had heard Sir Edw. Nevill say divers times, and sometimes [sing] merrily, that he trusted this world would amend and that honest men should rule one day, and that she had blamed him for so saying. Sir Edw. Nevill showed her that the King had sent Peter Meotes over sea to slay card. Pole with a hand gun. Signed: [Gertrude] Exeter.

9 Nov:—The said lady further says that when her husband went Northwards at the time of the insurrection, Sir Edw. Nevell came to her and said, "Madam, how do you? Be you merry?" She replied, "How can I be merry? My lord is gone to battle, and he will be one of the [foremost]." Sir Edward said again, "Madame, be not afeared of this, nor of the second, but beware of the third." Examinate said again to him, "[Ah] Mr. Nevell, you will never leave your Welsh prophecies, but one day this will turn you to displeasure."

12 Nov:—She further says that she has heard Sir Edward sing in her garden at Horsley that Peter Meotes was gone over seas to kill Card. Pole. She also said she had heard him say many times in the said garden [that he] trusted [knaves should be] put down and lords should reign on[e day].

[item 765]

Statements by Gervase Tyndall concerning Margaret, Countess of Salisbury

Information against her by Gervase Tyndall otherwise named Clifton.

* * * oftes wold be no ... be none ther abowtes [of the new ler]ny[n]ge as the callyt but that my lady scholde by and [by dismiss] them under same other coler and pretens for the ... Ester was a twelmonth x or xij off my lord Montygu [se]rvantes went to Cychester to be confessyd, with the which thyng [my] lady was not a Iytyll dyscontent. Otf thys thynge he sayd [h]e had good wyttnes.

"[I]f my lord] wyll take the payns to examane stratly and severally Mr. Newtone and Mr. Nycollsune, schaplayns to my lady, and specyally Newton, I [dowt] thynk suerly he schall come to the knollyge off [much fals spakyng a monge them, for thes be the ryngleders [of] my ladys error all together, as I well persaved be the wysperyng off the holle hows all moste, when the cam to the surgan hows, for I never came with yn her gates as long as I lay at Warblyngtun. nor never was bedone ons to drynke."

... was Rycharde Ayer at surgery my lady off Salsbery ... [w]ch dwelythe at Warblyngtun, he came at certayne tym [unto] me and sayd that he had ben resunynge with the curat off [Ha]vonde, which he sayd and aflermyd was skasly the Kyngys [fr]end, but he wolde not tell the caws why. Also he accusyd [t]he curat of Warblyngtun for revelynge of hys confessone; which, as [he] atfermyd, askte hym forgevunes afterward off hys knes. Note with [st]ondynge he sayd ther wer a company off prestes [in] my lady's howse. which dyd her muche harme and kepte her [from] the trewe knolyche of God's Word. Howe it chansyd I [can]e not tell, but thes Rychard sayd un to me, Ye muste departe, [J]eruas Tyndel, my lady hys note contente with me that ... yowe ar her, for as muche as sche ys credabully ynfor[me]d that yowe ar all of the newe lernynge. Then I [an]swerd and sayd I wolde not departe, notber for lord [nor] lady, tyll I were letter amendyd. Then he sayd with[in] a day or ij after that my lady had commayndyd hym [to send]e away all hys patyentes frome hys hows. Then I askyd [hym] ernystly what schold be the caws, and he sayd so that [I wo]lde kepyt closse he wolde tell me; which I promysyd [to] hym. Then he sayd the prestes yn my ladys kold not ... yn with me yn any wys. Then I answerd and sayd, I pray [you] brenge me to communycatyon with sume off them. Then [he] sayd the wer suche closse knaves that the wold nether resune [net]her be resand with. Fordermor he sayd that yff yt wern[ot] Howsse which he dewe[lleth] ... also he lobord ... he wolde netulle a sorte off them that the schold s ... Then I sayd, Kolde yowe so doe. Wher un[to he answerd] and sayd that ther was falsse packyng a[mong them], which when I ynstantly desyerd to knoe, he sayd [to me], Yff I wer as wel aquantyd with my lord Prevysele as [he] hys I wold tell hym a tale that wher worth t[ell]ylge. Then I sayd yif be wold so dooe I wolde g ... yowe and brynge yowe to a kynsmane off myn whoss [name] ys Gerom Lyn, other els to Master Moryson, which was [sum] tym petycanom with me in my lordes Cardynall Colly[ge at] Oxforde, which bothe I affermyd wold brynge by[m to] my lordes gras and caws hym to be harde; ye, and moro[ver] that my lord wold geve hym gret thankes yn th[at] behalff, and do mor for hym then ever my lady w[old]. Then he answerde and sayd very secratly theis w[ords]: Tyndall, her ys a knave which dewelythe by, wos n[ame ys] Hewe Holand, and he begenyths nowe off late [to act] the marchant mane and the broker, for he go[yth over] the see and convays letters to Master Helyar ower [parson] her off Warblyntune (which I thynke he affermy[d to be at] Orlyans), and he playthe the knave off thother [hand] and convaythe letters to Master Poole the Cardy[nall, and] all the secretes off the rein off Ynglond ys k[nowyn to the] bychope off Rome as well as th ... wer her.

Then I sayd, Doe yowe knoe thes for a cer[ten] ... is send for o ... was at [han] ... coome to a certain man hows whos nam ys Westmel (?) ... synger sayd that the caws was that I schold have a [pupil o]r ij to ynstructyn the Latyn tonge, but yt was for no [ot] her caws but to confond me, for as moche as the prestes had [re]

portyd that I was an Observant Frere, for the had gotune [an]
obstynate frer amonge them, which was send for for the moste ...
[t]o put me to lake and schame; which thynge when I persavyd [I]
declaryd my selff to be no suche parsne and defyde them all which
are frers. When I had so done, the curat, Sir Wyllyam Wantlatyn
was most bese (busy), and askyd why many [persons] callyd me
Tyndall and sume Clyftun; and I answerd and sayd that my uncull,
Doctor Clyftun, which gave me exybition yn Oxford nammyd me
after that nam, and thys thynge Master Moresun kane wyttnes,
that many callyd me so yn Oxford after hym, and at the last I troe
I callyd thys which schold be a prest knave and bade hym remember
Rychard Ayers wordes, which were that he scholde scassly be the
Kyngis frend. And when I sayd soe, by and by yn a gret fewme one
[B]owcher the constabull, which was present, answerd and sayd,
[I] wold thowe scholdes knoyt that I and xx moe wyll coome [u]p
and testyfy for hym, and yt was mery yn thes contry [be] for suche
felowys came, which fyndythe suche fawtes with ower honestes
prestes. Then I spake and sayd, Master Constabull, what mene
yowe to be so hasty? Yt had been yower parte tofor to have askyd
whether I myself had knone any almost ... I were wake sprytyd
and sayd morove[r] ... hard thes words as paraventure the schold,
th ... what he menythe be thes words, y[t was mery] yn ower
contry befor suche felowys camynhyt, which fy[ndythe] suche
faytes, and sayd Haunschyer was a quiat contry ... the sumthynge
a frayd off thes wordes, yn as muche a[s. .] rehersyd them the next
day follyng went strei[ght to] Sir Geffera Pooll, which send for me
and askyd why I [did] say thes wordes. Also he bad me spek yff
I kneue a[ny] thynge, for he sayd he was the Kynge justyce and ...
frynd, and I declaryd thes matter befor rehersyd and sayd the mygt
say so welynoug for yt ys truth.

"Testes Johanes Ansard : N. Westme ...

"Rychard Ayer sayd that ther colde be nothynge be done, nether
s ... yn all [the country] wer he dwellyd bout my Lady dyd knoe yt,
all thow [yt wer] never so secret yn mens hartes for the curat dyd
reuell ... *sub sigillo secreto* as the papystes sae the may doe to my

Lady, and the acordynge to ther owthe wysp[drd] yn my Ladvs eer, saynge that the myght so doe, for as muche ... for the sole helthe off the partys yn that my Lady was off g[ood mind] and wold se secret reformatyon and feyn as thowe sche dyd [know] be sume other mens; and thys was for no other caus as ... e Master Tyndail, yff yowe chanse to have commu[nicacion with a] certayn mane whom my Lady pote owte oft sevvys ... lernyng. he wyll tell more then thys, whos name ... crese maker, with whome when I went to Hauond from [Richa]rd Avers hows which was at Warblyntune, I mett with and I ... rd hys a quantans for as moche as I parsavyd that he favord [gre]tly also Godes word. Then he sayd the same to me, and so after [said] unto me ther aI yntendyd to teche a gramer scoll ... man with me off the scryptur, but we agred to well hare ... e dysputatyon. Then he sayd unto me, Have yowe good a [quant]ans yn my lord Prevysel hows? To whom I answred and sayd [that I] hade. Then he sayd Ye may doe a good ded to pootforthe suche [things] as I cold ynfonne yowe off. Then I sayd, [Have] yowe nonaquantans. and ar the prynce gras sarvand? Then he [sayd, Y]es, I am aqnantyd with Master Cottnne, whome I have movyd [in t]hys matter, and whate concell he gave hym I do not well re[mem]ber boot as farforthe as my memory wyll sarave me, Master [Cottune] movyd hyme to lettyt a lone and besenote (busy not) hym self with such [thyngees for]other men schold do yt welynowhe yff the mychgt parsa[ve them to] be trewethus. I askyd hym what the matter [was]. Then he sayd, Tyndall. whatt a thynge ys thys? [My la]dy off Salsberys consell schall command oponly yn [the Kyng]es [name that no mane so hardy which be her tennantes schall occopy [books of] the Newe Testament yn Englych or any other new [books] which the Kynges Hynes hathe pryrelyged; which he affennyd [he had] good wyttnes off. Mor over he sayd that the parsune off Warblyngtnn wh[ose name] ys Helyar ass[ured hym] that the Byschope off Rome had as m[any friends] yn England as ever he had, not withstandy[ng the new] acte, savynge yn on poynte; morover perse ... he was supremhed over all the chorch o[ff Christ] : which opynyon, when thes forsayd

Peter sayd yt [was] tresone, the parsnnne fled to Portamothe, and ther wa[s] vj days yn Henry Bykyls hows, tyll such tym as he was c[um] yn to a schep which went yn to Franse, which he sayd w[as a] thynge opunde to my lord Pryvysel, and so hys goodes [was taken], but Sir Geffera Pooll and Master Pallet mayd suc[h] scheft that the matter was clokyd and hys good[es re]stauryd again; but not with standynge he sayd that y[ff he] myght talke with lord Prevy Sell he wold so d[iscover] the matter that the schold no lenger blynd [hym] yn hyt as the had done. Mor over he sayd that the cu[rate] of Warblyngtune left owt the dedaratyone off pa[rpos] when he red the Kyng's book. Also the b ... sayd that thys Hewe Holand and Henry Bykyls and ... Standyche, clarke off the kechyn to my lady, wher [such] crafty felows that nay lord schold never get nothy[ng of] them, except he had ther concell and went [more] wysly to worke.

[item 817]

Statements of Hugh Holland

The examination of Hugh Holland, taken 3 Nov. 30 Hen. VIII. Hugh Holland, late of the parish of Warblington, Hants, says that in the beginning of summer was three or four years, he, Sir Geoffrey Pole, and the vicar of Est Mayn, with their servants, went together into the Isle of Wight, and when at sea the vicar said to him, "This is a good weather to go to the seas. I would gladly go to Amyas. How sayest thou, Hugh? Dost thou know the way?" He said, "Yea," and the vicar said "Will you go with me?" Said he would if his master, Sir Geoffrey Pole, would give him leave.

"I warrant you he will," said the vicar; and after returning, Sir Geoff. Pole at his own house asked this examinate whether he would go with the vicar of Est Mayn over sea or not. Replied that he would go if he bade him. "Yes," said Sir Geoffrey, "I will desire you and [com]mand you too; for he will go to Amyas and I think to Paris, to study there, and will tarry at Paris and not return with you. But that is no matter to you: whether he tarry there or come again he shall honestly recompense you." On this, at the end of the summer examinate hired a French ship, and at Portsmouth shipped the said vicar with his servant, Henry Pyning, two horses, and 36*l.* in money, besides goods of his own, and landed at Newhaven. Then went in company with the vicar to Paris, and there left him in company of two English scholars named Reynolds and Bucklar. Being asked what communication he had with the vicar by the way, says the vicar told him he was glad he was over sea, for if he had tarried in England he feared he should have been put to death; for he considered the ordinances of England were against God's law. He said he had departed secretly, partly because my lady of Salisbury would not give him leave, partly because his mother, if she had known it, would have been much grieved. Being asked whether the said vicar at that going over wrote letters or sent messages to anyone in England, replies that he sent from Newhaven letters by a Frenchman to Mr. G. Pole, but examinate does not know the contents. After deponent's return he told the said Sir Geoffrey how he had brought the vicar to Paris; for which Sir Geoffrey thanked him and promised he should not lack while he lived. Also, after the fruits of the vicar's benefices were sequestrated Sir Geoffrey sent for him and promised him 40s. to carry letters to him to Paris; which he did and brought others home from the said vicar to Sir William Paulet, then Comptroller, Dr. Stuarde, Chancellor to the bp. of Winchester, and to Sir Geoffrey Pole, and a little writing to the vicar's brother-in-law, John Fowell of Warbington (sic), to whom he delivered also all the other letters to be conveyed to those men they were sent to. After this, about Easter was two years, this examinate having business of his own at Antwerp, the said John Fowell went with him, and they both went together to Louvain, where the said vicar then was; but he carried no letters or message to or from him, and whether Fowell carried any he knows not. Fowell has since been twice over sea with the said vicar, sent on one occasion about this time twelve months by Mr. Pole, but for what cause he knows not, except that he said he was sent to learn whether the vicar had any letters to send to England. The vicar was at that time gone from Louvain—to cardinal Pole, as examinate thinks. Another time, Sir William Paulet sent the said Fowell to Louvain for a certificate from the University of his being there, to the intent that the sequestration might be released. Further, after Easter was twelve months, hearing that wheat sold well in Flanders, deponent loaded a ship with wheat to go thither, when Sir Geoff. Pole sent for him and said, "I hear say you intend to go into Flanders. [My] brother, I hear say, is in those parts. Will you [do] me an errand unto him?" Deponent agreed, and Sir Geoffrey said to him, "I pray you commend me to my brother and show him I would I were with him, and will come to him if he will have me; for show him the world in England waxeth all crooked, God's law is turned upso-down, abbeys and churches overthrown, and he is taken for a traitor; and I think they will cast down parish churches and all at the last. And because he shall trust you, show him this token, and show him also that Mr. Wilson and Powell be in the Tower yet, and show him further that there be sent from England daily to destroy him, and that much money would be given for his head, and that the lord Privy Seal said openly in the Court that he, speaking of the said Cardinal, should destroy himself well enough, and that Mr. Brian and Peter Meotes was sent into France to kill him with a hand-gun or otherwise as they should see best." He farther says that the day before he departed Sir Geoffrey sent for him and met with him upon Portsdown, and said, "How sayest thou, Hugh, if I go over with thee myself and see that good fellow?" meaning his brother the Cardinal Replied, "Nay, Sir, my ship is fully loaded, and the mariners be not meet for this purpose." "Well," said Sir Geoffrey, "then I pray you remember what I have said unto you and fare you well." After this he passed the seas and sold his wheat at Nieuport, and from thence went to Cambray; and because cardinal Pole had gone thence to an abbey called Anno, 40 English miles beyond Cambray, he took his journey thither, where he met one Throkmarton, servant to the Cardinal, who asked if he came from England. Replied, Yes. "From the King?" asked Throkmarton. He answered, "No." "From my lady of Salisbury?" "No," said this examinate, "I came from Sir Geoffrey

Pole." Throkmarton then went up into the abbey and told the Cardinal, who after mass sent for deponent into the church, where he delivered his message to him. The Cardinal then said, "And would my lord Privy Seal so fain kill me? Well, I trust it shall not lie in his power. The King is not contented to bear me malice himself, but provoketh other against me, and hath written to the French king that he should not receive me as cardinal or legate; but yet I was received into Paris better than some men would." He said he knew that Mr. Brian and Peter Meotes had been sent for that purpose, but he trusted it should not lie in their powers. He asked examinate of those bishops in England who were named honest men. Answered that the bishops of London and Durham were so named. "Nay," said the Cardinal; "the bishop of London, I think, is an honest man, but the bishop of Durham is none." Being asked why he thought them honest, he said because he saw his master, Sir Geoffrey, often resorting to them to dinners and suppers. The Cardinal afterwards said, "Commend me to my lady my mother by the same token that she and I looking upon a wall togethers read this, *Spes mea in Deo est*, and desire her blessing for me. I trust she will be glad of mine also; and if I wist that she were of the opinion that other bee ther, mother as she is myn, I wold treade uppon h[er] with my feete. Commend me to my lord my brother by this token, *In Domino confido*, and to my brother Sir Geoffrey, and bid him meddle little and let all things alone." Had no other message to or from the said Cardinal to anyone. If any other thing come to his remembrance will not fail to open it. Being asked what message he had from any other about the said Cardinal, answers that Throkmarton desired his commendations to the lord Montacute by the token that they had communed together at his last being in England in a place which he now remembers not, and bade him be contented till his coming into England. Further, he says that on coming home he delivered all the messages to Sir Geoffrey Pole and showed nothing to lady Salisbury or lord Montacute, because Sir Geoffrey told him not to do so; for he said his brother, lord Montacute, was out of his mind, and would show all to the lord

Privy Seal. He further says that since that time, especially before the King's coming into Sussex, Sir Geoffrey often pressed him to go over sea again and to take him with him, for he doubted not they should both live merrily there, and if he could but come to the bp. of Luke he should have money enough, and he trusted once to kiss the Pope's feet, and he made many large promises to this examinate, but he always refused to go. Signed: Hou Hallond.

Holland afterwards said that about 12 months past he showed lord Montacute that Sir Geoff. Pole was very desirous to go over sea, and he marvelled much what he meant by it. "Marry," said the lord Montacute, "I charge you meddle not with that in any case." Being asked on what occasion he so conversed with lord Montacute; says he brought a pair of knives from a servant of the Cardinal's to John Walker, which were delivered him at Antwerp; and Montacute hearing of it communed with him of it. On which occasion he showed him as above, but told him nothing of his communication with the Cardinal. Signed.

Further deposition, 11 Nov.

Says he brought home letters from the vicar of Est Mayn containing a little "skroe," intimating that if Sir Geoffrey Pole would convey any letters to him he might deliver them to one Monteys, servant with the Emperor's ambassador. He says also that because Sir Geoffrey, a little before the King's coming into Sussex, was very importunate with this examinate to go over sea, he showed it to Thos. Standish, servant to my lady of Salisbury, praying him to inform lord Montacute, telling Standish at the same time that he had been with cardinal Pole, and that the said Sir Geoffrey showed him at such times as he stirred this examinate to go over seas that lord Montacute would as fain be over as he. Signed.

Further examination of Hugh Holland.

Hugh Holland, on further examination, says that when he came from beyond sea after having spoken with cardinal Poole, one

Babham, steward to the lady of Salisbury, came to this examinate's house at Warblington and said 'What, Hugh! have you spoken with that traitor my Lady's son?' Answered 'Nay.' Then said Babham, 'You have spoken with some of his servants.' 'Yea,' said this examinate, 'I have spoken with Throkmerton.' 'Marry,' said Babham, 'I advise you keep that secret; it may hap to cost you your life else.' Signed.

[item 797]

Statements of Jerome Ragland

Jerom Raglande, examined, [says] lord Montacue, his master, showed him a copy of letters from Reynold [Pole] to the bp. of Durham of "four or five [sheets] of paper," in answer to a letter from the Bishop. Forgets the contents of this letter; Montacue afterwards burned it at Bokmer. Wished to save the same from burning in order to learn the contents. Heard the letter read in presence of Montacue, Mr. Colyns, and himself. Has often heard Montacue murmur at the state of the world and the King's proceedings. [*Marginal note*: "The first article."] Montacue feared further mischief, and that such as ruled about the King would mar all. Told Colyns of a book which cardinal Pole had [written] against the King commencing *Quid dicam aut quid faciam* but never saw the book : Babham told him at Bokmer the book began so. Has often heard Montacue lament the death of lord Burgavenny. [*Marginal note*: Affirmeth the saying of Sir Geoffrey Pole.] At the time of the Insurrection, Montacue said "Now if my lord a Burgavenny were alive, he were able to make a great number of men in Kent and Sussex"; and often said Burgavenny was "a noble man and assured friend." Tyrell has gone between Montacue and the lord Marquis often : knows not if he carried letters. Has seen a big fellow in a tawny coat come to Montacue from the Marquis, but knows not on what errand. Has heard Montacue lament the pulling down of abbeys—especially Bisham— and say he trusted to see Bisham abbey in as good state as ever. Has heard him lament the Marquis' sickness and gout, and say the Marquis was the "most passionate and impatient man in his sickness that ever he knew." Has heard say (but of whom he cannot tell), it were a meet marriage for Reynold Pole to have the Lady Mary, the King's daughter. Last summer being [sent] by Montacute to Eliz. Darell [ab]out assurance of certain lands, she said Mr. Wyatt was [come] out of Spain, where he had been highly entertained, and that Mr. Wyatt said they had a poison in Spain, which put on an arrow head, and the same pricking any person, he should die, and the remedy was the juice of a quince or peach. She also said Mr. Wyatt saw cardinal Pole, "but he spake not with him, nor one of them would not look on another."Mr. Wyatt had told the King about the poison and asked if he should bring any hither, but the King answered "Nay." Signed: Jerom Ragland.

Further examined, says that after the Insurrection, when it was said the King had promised the Northern men to hold a parliament at York for satisfaction of their articles, and it was known the King would not [go to] the North for that purpose, Montacute said "In tym[es] past King's words [would] be believed, but nowadays they be used for.....e, wherefore if the Commons do rise again th[ey wi]ll trust no fair promise nor words." Lord Mowntagew had all Mr. More's books......... volume (?), and did much take pleasu[re in rea]ding of them. Hugh Hol[ande] at Warblington desired to speak with lord Montague, and said "he must needs" speak with him. Deponent said, "Tell [it to] me and I will tell my lord." Holland said it was that Sir Geoffrey Pole must needs go over sea, unless Montague found a remedy. [*Marginal note*: Confirms Holland's saying.] Reported this to Montague and he thereupon spoke with Holland at Bokmer, but deponent knows not what was said.

Pp. 5. Stained and mutilated. In Cromwell's hand. With marginal notes by Ric. Pollard upon the character of the evidence.

Headed: "the xxviij [day of October?]"

Jerome Regland further examined, says, lord Mon[tacute sai]d the acts which the King caused to be made in Parliament were very cruelly made, such as the Act of Treason, &c, and if he were of the Council he would, notwithstanding those Acts, advise a charitable punishment so that men should not die therefor. Shortly after the Insurrection, lord M. showed him at Bokmer that if that matter (the Northern party) had been "man handelyd" it would have been well enough. Lord M. showed him at Bokmer 12 months past, "that he hath seen more gentleness and benignity in times past at the King's hands than he doth nowadays,"and said two years ago that knaves ruled about the King, and if be lived to see a change of the world, they should "have punishment for their offences without cruelty." Has heard lord M. say at Bokmer two years ago, and both before and since, that "If this world come to a change we shall have somewhat to do." Heard lord M. say at Bisham about two years past, that the King had said to all the lords, that if they would not do what he moved them to do "he would forsake them and go with the Lubekks; and the lord M said then also that then we should be well rid of him."(*In margin*: Knows not what it was that the King moved the lords). Lord M. showed him as Bokmer two years past that he could trust few men nowadays. Lord M. showed him that "the lord Marquis is a noble man." Thinks be had great trust in the lord Marquis of Exeter. (*In margin*: Against the lord Marquis.) Heard lord M. say once or twice at Bokmer two or three years ago, "We shall lack nothing so much one day as honest men." Heard lord M. say "the King is full of flesh and unwieldly, and that he cannot long continue with his sore leg." Lord M. showed him that peradventure the King would send him [over se]es for his affairs, and then he would do the best service he could, but if he failed he would tarry over seas till England was in a better state. Heard Lord M. at "Okyngham [Bramsell] heth" this summer, wish himself and his son were over seas with six persons more whom he did not name. Has heard lord M. say his brother Sir Geoffrey Pole shall not serve the King. Has heard lord M. within this 12 months praise his brother the Cardinal in his learning and in his living, and say he thought him ordained by God to do good. Lord M. told him a year past, "the King hath a sort of k[nav]es in his privy chamber about him." Read a letter from cardinal Pole to lord M. about three years past, containing "that he would send shortly a great horse to the lord M.; and also he advertised the lord Montegu that he should [bring] up his son himself in activity; and also that the revolutions in Italy declareth great war to be in those parts shortly." Heard lord M. say two years past "the King never made man but he destroyed him again either with displeasure or with the sword." Lord M. told him three years past he liked not many of the bishops. Was trusted by lord M. About three years past when lord M. began to recover from his sickness, he sent examinate to Horsley to show the lord Marquis of his recovery: the lord Marquis said he was glad thereof. (*In margin*: Against the lord Marquis.) Heard Perkyns, servant to lord M.. say, "that it were ...... marriage betwixt my lady Mary and the cardinal Pole."

Pp.5. The first paragraph in Cromwell's hand. All the rest, except the last article, in Ric. Pollard's. Each page has been signed at the bottom "Thomas Crumwell," but this is crossed out and the signature "Jerom Ragland" substituted. Endd.

Hiero[me Raglan]de, [further] examined. Has known lord Montacute, his master, often resort to the marquis of Exeter to his houses at Horseley and London, but knows not for what causes. Tyrell has gone to the Marquis from lord Montacute, aud when asked by this examinate sometimes said he went thither and sometime answered nothing. "Sterkey once showed this examinate that cardinal Poole was m[ad] to come into [England] France, for he will have a ... in his way Sir Francis Bryan, Peter Meotes or Wing[field] . , . yn over to rid him." Showed this, on coming home, to lord Montacute, who said he knew that well enough. Has often seen lord Montacute and Colyns alone together in the garden at Bukmar and in the woods adjoining, and in the place called the Long Rowe. Has known Montacute and Sir Geoffrey Pole walk together in the garden at Bockmar and in the great chamber, and has known Montacute, Sir Geoffrey and Colyns all to walk together in the garden. Colyns was sent about Corpus Christi last to Sir Geoffrey's house to burn certain letters in the study there. Thinks Montacute was privy to his going. Colins, on his return, said he had burned the letters. Hugh Holland to[ld examinate] that he feared Sir Geoffrey would go beyond seas, and that he had spoken with Bernardine, cardinal Pole's servant, and brought a pair of knives for a token to John Walker.

[item 702]

Statements of Oliver Franckeleyn

Oliver Franckeleyn, examined 20 Nov. 30 Hen. VIII, says that hearing Hugh Holland had carried the vicar of Est Mayn over seas he asked him whether it was true. Holland said that he had brought him over seas to Paris to school. Examinate answered, "I pray God his going over do no hurt." Says also that perceiving Holland frequently went over seas he said to him once, "I pray God all be well ye run so oftentimes over seas." Holland answered "The vicar of Est Mayne hath made me his factor and the lord Privy Seal knoweth that [he] is in Louvain at school, and is contented that I shall make his exchange for him." Says also that half a year ago or so, because the priest of Havant and one Wysedom had showed Sir Geoffrey Poole that they had been told by one Tyndall that Hugh Holland had been over seas with letters from the lady of Sarum and the said Sir Geoffrey Poole to the vicar of Est Mayne, Sir Geoffrey Poole showed this examinate of it. On which, the matter being inquired into [by] the bailey of Havant and nothing appearing, the said Sir Geoffrey, by counsel of this examinate, took the said Hugh Holland and one Ayer with him, and rode to the Lord Privy Seal; and at his return the said Sir Geoffrey showed this examinate that the lord Privy Seal was good lord to him and had despatched the said Ayar and Holland. Has heard divers men say since Reynold Poole was made Cardinal, "He shall be pope one day"; but cannot tell who said so. Has admonished lady Salisbury to beware of Sir Geoffrey Poole, saying, "I pray God, Madame, he do you no hurt one day." And being examined why, he replies, Not that he knew of any purpose of his to go over seas, "but because his stomach gave him (he knoweth not wherefor) that the said Sir Geoffrey should one day turn her to displeasure." Being asked what answer she made, says she said, "I trow he is not so unhappy that he will hurt his mother, and yet I care neither for him, nor for any other, for I am true to my Prince." Asked at what time he gave her this warning, says it was since Sir Geoffrey hurt himself in the Tower.

[item 875]

APPENDIX 2

MARGARET'S GOODS AND SERVANTS

These inventories, taken on 14–15 November 1538, are abstracted in *Letters and Papers*, Foreign and Domestic, Henry VIII, Volume 13 Part 2, August–December 1538. Footnotes and footnote references have been removed; otherwise, the editorial emendations have not been altered. The more complete inventories can be found in Hazel Pierce's doctoral dissertation.

R. O. Inventory taken at Warblington, 14 Nov. 30 Hen. VIII, of the furniture in the following chambers, viz.: —the wardrobe, the middle and lower chambers over the gate, the nether and uppermost corner chamber, the two bedchambers, the low parlour next the great parlour, the great chamber, the next chamber called the waiting chamber, the dining chamber, the chambers of Mr. Stuarde, Mr. Chamlay, Sir Robert, Mr. Nicholson, the clerk, George Mysse and Harry Somers, the cook, John Hode and Harry Latymer, Edm. Thurlowe, Thope and Davy, the porter, the comptroller's servant, Mr. Newburghe, Mr. Warnay and Mr. Middileton, Mr. Parkyns and Mr. Hasset, Broune and Cotismour, the groom of the stables, the baker, John Pistowe, in my Lady's own chamber and the chamber within it, in the chapel chamber and closet, in the chapel, in the middle chamber in the tower over my Lady's chamber, in the great parlour, the ewry, kitchen, scullery, and buttery. "The apparel in her guardrobe," i.e., 1 gown black satin furred with "bowge"; 1 gown black satin furred with martens, sleeves lined with sable; 1 gown black velvet lined with buckram, sleeves with satin; a suit of foynes for a woman's gown, the sleeves martens; 1 kirtle tawny velvet; 1 old kirtle tawny damask; 2 small cloth sacks, 7½ tod of wool, and a "botle sadle coverd with buff." An "estimate view" of the remainder in all offices, including farm stock at Warblington, Crockham, and Dorford.

Inventory made 15 Nov. 30 Hen. VIII. by the lord Admiral and bishop of Ely, of the goods of the lady of Sarum:—
Coffers at Warblington which the said lords have sealed and left with John Chadreton and John Babham, steward to the said lady; one of them contains silk and gold to work with, another silk "to set the young a-work and a cushion wrought with the needle," another linen and a case of knives silver and gilt, with a. little cup of mother-of-pearl, and so on. (2.) Coffers brought from Warblington to Cowdrey, and there left sealed, i.e., a black carriage chest, the little chest of "seo" with a chequier in the top, the great red carriage chest, containing numerous items of plate (detailed). Of all the coffers my Lady has the keys and the said lords have sealed them.

    (3.) Stuff my Lady has to serve her at Cowdrey. Md. besides the "said money" in the leather bag and the crimson velvet purse there is found in the coffers of the said lady 20l. delivered to John Chadreton to serve the household at Warblington, and 6 silver spoons to be occupied there. Besides the plate at Cowdrey there was pledged to the steward, Babham, 2 standing cups and 1 doz. trenchers of silver, and to the comptroller, Oliver Franklayne, a salt of gold and 6 silver bowls.

The names of her servants.
The lady Margaret Stafford, Mrs. Wenefred, Mary and Margaret Poole, daughters of Sir Arthur, Katharine Poole, daughter of

Sir Geoffrey, Johan Cholmeley, Johan Francleyne, Anne Raglande, Eliz. Cheynye, Dorothy Erneley, and Alice Densell. John Babham, steward, Oliver Frankleigne, comptroller; Mr. Newton, Mr. Nicholson, and Sir Robt. Backhouse, chaplains; Geo. Vernay, Wm. Perkyns, Chr. Newburgh, Edw. Middleton, Walt. Browne and Ant. Cotismor, gentlemen waiters; John Larke and Thos. Tandishe (sic) clerks of the kitchen. Also 6 yeomen of the chamber, marshal and usher, and servants in the pantry 2, buttery 2, ewry 2, wardrobe 2, Harry Roberts at Bisham, porters 2, grooms of the chamber 2, cooks 3, and bakers 2; all named. Also a slaughterer, a "catour," a tyler, a beer brewer, 3 boys of the kitchen, a horsekeeper, servant of the "squillery," almoner and laundress, all likewise named.

"Gentlemen's servants," 10; viz., Babham 2, Frankleigne 2, Newton 1, Nicholson 1, Geo. Verney 1, Perkynz 1, Newburgh 1, and Cotismor 1.

Harry Corbet, found of alms; and the fool. Total, 72.

[item 838].

NOTES

Abbreviations

CPR   Calendar of the Patent Rolls
CSP, Milan   Calendar of State Papers, Milan
CSP, Spain   Calendar of State Papers, Spain
CSP, Venice   Calendar of State Papers, Venice
LL   The Lisle Letters
LP   Letters and Papers
Pierce, MP   Hazel Pierce, *Margaret Pole, Countess of Salisbury 1473–1541*
PROME   Parliament Rolls of Medieval England

1 *Daughter of Violence*

1. Rous, no. 58.
2. Crowland, p. 143.
3. Society of Antiquaries, Collection of Ordinances, pp. 87–103.
4. Rous, no. 58; Lander, pp. 247–48; Hicks, 124–25; Dugdale, v. 2, p. 64.
5. Calendar of Patent Rolls 1466–85, p. 212.
6. Pierce, MP, p. 6.
7. PROME, January 1484, item 1(5).
8. Pierce, MP, p. 8.
9. Mancini, 88.
10. Sutton and Hammond, p. 270.
11. Mancini, p. 93.
12. Rous, no. 60.
13. Sutton and Visser-Fuchs, pp. 32–34.
14. Vergil, ch. 26, para. 1; Pierce, MP, p. 11.

2 *A New Order*

1. Campbell, vol. 1, p. 311; Pierce, MP, pp. 11–12.
2. Cavell, p. 103.
3. Chrimes, p. 51.
4. Chrimes, p. 59.
5. *ODNB*, 'John de la Pole, Earl of Lincoln'; Bennett, pp. 37–38.
6. For a concise account of this confusing episode, see *ODNB*, 'Lambert Simnel'.
7. Vergil, ch. 26, para. 7.
8. For what follows see Pierce, 'King's Cousin'.
9. Underwood and Jones, p. 31.
10. Nichols, *Collectanea Topographica and Genealogica*, vol. 1, p. 21.
11. CSP, Spain, vol. 1, item 210.
12. Cavell, pp. 131–59.
13. Cavell, pp. 159, 164.
14. Pierce, King's Cousin, p. 192–93, 205; Pierce, MP, p. 18.
15. Pierce, MP, pp. 22–23.
16. Pierce, King's Cousin; Chrimes, p. 140.
17. Arthurson, p. 6.
18. For what follows, see *ODNB*, 'Perkin Warbeck', 'Edward, styled Earl of Warwick'; Arthurson.
19. Arthurson, p. 199.
20. Hall, p. 490.
21. Hall, p. 491.
22. CSP, Spain, vol. 1, item 239.
23. Gairdner, vol. 1, pp. 113–14.
24. Statutes of the Realm, vol. 3, p. 100.

3 *Two Widows*

1. Pollard, vol. 1, p. 206–08.
2. Morgan-Guy, pp. 54–55.
3. Kipling, pp. 5, 42, 77–78.
4. Kipling, pp. 79–80.
5. Houlbrooke, pp. 71–72.
6. Pierce, MP, 17, 18, 28–29, 'King's Cousin', 224.
7. Pierce, MP, pp. 18, 28–30. Somerset, who later became the Earl of Worcester, was the son of Henry Beaufort, Duke of Somerset, executed by Edward IV after the Battle of Hexham in 1464.
8. For what follows see Powell, Sue, 'Margaret Pole and Syon Abbey'.
9. Phillips, vol. 1, p. 5.
10. Spedding, p. 260.

4 *Countess of Salisbury*

1. More, 130–31.
2. Starkey, pp. 244–45.
3. Starkey, pp. 304–09.
4. Pierce, MP, p. 32; LP, vol. 1, item 82.
5. Hall, pp. 508–09.
6. LP, vol. 1, No. 158(19).
7. CSP, Venice, vol. 5, item 525.
8. Mayer, *Reginald Pole*, pp. 172–73.
9. Loades, *Tudor Court*, p. 138.
10. Statutes of the Realm, p. 100.
11. For what follows see Pierce, MP, pp. 35–40.
12. Wright, p. 195.
13. Powell, Edgar, pp. xii, xviii.
14. Kingsford, pp. 28–31, 50–51.
15. Goodall, p. 413 pl. 309.
16. Longcroft, pp. 117–18.
17. Pierce, MP, p. 197 n.48; Pierce, dissertation, pp. 356–74.
18. For the distinction between types of fools, see Southworth, pp. 5–6.
19. Harris, *English Aristocratic Women*, p. 39.
20. Pierce, MP, 60–61, 82, 83.
21. Pierce, MP pp. 82–83.
22. Pierce, MP, p. 17; VCH Hampshire, vol. 5, 'Christchurch (Christchurch Twyneham): Churches and charities'; Perkins, pp. 117–18; LP, vol. 14(2), item 627.
23. LP, vol. 1, items 234, 609, 774, 957, 1192; Brears, pp. 124–25.
24. LP, vol. 1, item 2137(5).
25. Pierce, MP, p. 46; Miller, p. 9.
26. Pierce, MP, pp. 50–51, 200 n. 104.
27. Pierce, HP, pp. 74–75; Beccadelli, p. 157.
28. Pierce, MP, pp. 47–49. This Henry Pole was dead by 1543 or 1544. *ODNB*, 'Margaret Pole'.
29. *ODNB*, 'Sir Geoffrey Pole'; Pierce, MP, p. 52.
30. Pierce, MP, pp. 52–54; Harris, Edward Stafford, pp. 55–57; Historical Manuscript Commission, Seventh Report, p. 584.
31. Schenk, pp. 3–7; *ODNB*, 'Reginald Pole'.

5 *Lady Governess*

1. LP, vol. 2, item 1573.
2. Pierce, MP, p. 43.
3. Richardson, pp. 131–32, 136; LP, vol. 3, item 870.

4. McIntosh, *From Heads of Household*, pp. 10–11 (bracketed emendations in McIntosh).

5. Harris, Edward Stafford, p. 103.

6. Harris, Edward Stafford, p. 80.

7. Pierce, MP, p. 87.

8. LP, vol. 3, no. 1284(3).

9. Pierce, MP, pp. 87–90; LP Addenda vol. 1(1), no. 367.

10. Sneyd, pp. 125–31.

11. For this and the following paragraph see McIntosh, *Tudor Queenship*, p. 115; Pollnitz, pp. 131–32; Whitelock, pp. 29–30.

12. McIntosh, *From Heads of Household*, chapter 2.

13. Whitelock, pp. 30–31.

14. LP, vol. 4, item 1906.

15. Green, vol. 1, p. 309.

16. Harris, *English Aristocratic Women*, p. 46.

17. LP, vol. 4, item 2972.

18. Cooper, p. 96.

19. Pierce, MP, pp. 38, 90–91; LP, vol. 18(1), item 67.

20. For this and what follows, see Pierce, MP, pp. 91–97.

21. LP, vol. 4(2), item 4654.

22. Bernard, William Compton, p. 762.

23. Loades, Mary Tudor, pp. 46–47.

24. CSP, Milan, 1530, item 642.

25. LP, vol. 4, item 6586; Madden, p. 98.

26. Pierce, MP, pp. 65, 75.

27. LL, vol. 2, no. 174.

28. LL, vol. 3, no. 769.

29. CSP, Venice, vol. 4, item 682.

6 Perseverance

1. Williams, pp. 183–84.

2. Loades, *Henry VIII*, p. 109.

3. Williams, p. 243; Loades, *Henry VIII*, p. 182.

4. Werham, p. 111; Williams, pp. 253–54.

5. Quoted in Ives, p. 85.

6. CSP, Spain, vol. 3, pt. 2, item 113.

7. LP, vol. 4, intro. p. ccxlix.

8. CSP, Spain, vol. 3, pt. 2, item 131.

9. CSP, Spain, vol. 3 pt. 2, item 152.

10. Bernard, *King's Reformation*, p.8.

11. LP, vol. 4, items 4858, 4875.

12. Hall, pp. 754–55.

13. Tremlett, p. 265, and sources cited therein; Scarisbrick, p. 224.

14. For what follows see Cavendish, 79; CSP, Venice, vol. 4, item 482.

15. LP, vol. 4, item 5702.

16. LP, vol. 4, item 5734.

17. Scarisbrick, p. 227.

18. Scarisbrick, p. 236.

19. *ODNB*, 'Reginald Pole'; Mayer, 'Reginald Pole and the Parisian Theologians'; Mayer, *Reginald Pole*, pp. 54–55.

20. Pierce, MP, pp. 109–12: *ODNB*, 'Sir Geoffrey Pole', 'Henry Pole, Baron Montagu'; Williams, p. 301; Scarisbrick, p. 259.

21. *ODNB*, 'Wolsey, Thomas'; Fletcher, pp. 161–69.

22. CSP, Venice, vol. 4, item 584.

23. CSP, Spain, vol. 4 pt. 1, item 354.

24. Tremlett, p. 191; LP, vol. 4, item 6627; Kelly, p. 153.

25. LP, vol. 5, items 187 and 216.

26. Hall, p. 781; CSP, Spain, vol. 4 pt. 2, item 775.

27. CSP, Spain, vol. 4(2), item 778.

28. CSP, Spain, vol. 4(2), item 788.

7 Unheard-of Cruelty

1. CSP, Spain 4(2), item 880; Hall, p. 784.

2. For what follows see Mayer, *Reginald Pole*, pp. 56–61, *ODNB*, 'Reginald Pole'; Pierce, MP, pp. 109–10; Schenk, pp. 25–30; Mayer, *Correspondence*, vol. I, p. 69–70.

3. Mayer, *Reginald Pole*, p. 57.

4. CSP, Spain, vol. 4(2), item 1003.

5. Ives, pp. 160, 170.

6. Ives, p. 161; Bernard, *King's Reformation*, p. 67.

7. Ives, pp. 162–63, 170.

8. Bernard, *King's Reformation*, pp. 67–72.

9. CSP, Spain, vol. 4(2), items 1058, 1061.

10. CSP, Spain, vol. 4(2), item 1061.

11. Marius, pp. 438–39, Roper, pp. 33–34.

12. LP, vol. 6, items 562, 601; Norton, pp. 131, 135, 143.

13. *ODNB*, 'Henry Pole, Baron Montagu'.

14. LP, vol. 6, item. 1009.

15. Pierce, MP, p. 100; LP, vol. 6, item 1041.

16. LP, vol. 6, item 1126.

17. LP, vol. 6, item 1199.
18. CSP, Spain, vol. 4(2), item 1161.
19. Pierce, MP, pp. 103–04; *ODNB*, 'Elizabeth Barton'; LP, vol. 6, items 1464–65, 1468.
20. LP, vol. 8, item 263.
21. LL, vol. 2, no. 126.
22. LL, vol. 2, no. 136 and notes.
23. LL, vol. 2, nos. 113 and 145 and notes.
24. Gee and Harvey, pp. 242–43; Loades, *Cromwell*, p. 93.
25. LP, vol. 7, items 55, 391.
26. LL, vol. 2, no. 169; Rex, p. 72.
27. Bellamy, pp. 31–34.
28. Loades, Cromwell, pp. 109–10; Schofield, pp. 105–08.
29. LP, vol. 8, item 609.
30. LP, vol. 8, item 661.
31. CSP, Spain, vol. 5(1), item 156.
32. Bernard, *King's Reformation*, pp. 160–67; Schofield, pp. 107–08; *ODNB*, 'Sebastian Newdigate'; LP, vol. 8, items 886, 895.
33. For what follows see Bernard, 118–25; Fisher, John, *ODNB*; Loades, *Cromwell*, pp. 114–15; LP, vol. 8, items 948, 985.
34. Loades, Cromwell, p. 114; Schofield, p. 102, Bernard, *King's Reformation*, pp. 115–16.
35. CSP, Spain, vol. 4(2), item 1130.
36. CSP, Spain, vol. 5(1), item 231.
37. LP, vol. 8, item 974. For what follows see Center for Thomas More Studies, 'Trial of Sir Thomas More'.
38. Derrett, p. 455 n.2.
39. Stapleton, pp. 45–46. The original Latin letter can be found at the Center for Thomas More Studies' website.
40. Roper, p. 58.
41. Kelly, Karlin, and Wegemer, p. 20 n. 84.

8 Honour and Conscience

1. LP, v. 8, item 596; *ODNB*, 'William Barlow (d. 1568)'.
2. LL, vol. 2, nos. 412–13, 415, 419, 421; vol. 4, no. 836.
3. CSP, Spain vol. 4(2), item 1144; Fox, *Acts and Monuments*, 1570 ed., p. 1603.
4. LP, vol. 7, items 83, 296.
5. CSP, Spain, vol. 5(1), item 57.
6. LP, vol. 7, item 662.
7. LP, vol. 8, items 189, 200, 263.

8. LP, vol. 8, item 1105; Froude, *Divorce*, pp. 356–57; CSP, Spain, vol. 5(1), item 210.

9. CSP, Spain, vol. 5(1), item 218.

10. CSP, Spain, vol. 9, item 776.

11. LP, vol. 9, item 1036; vol. 10, item 59.

12. CSP, Spain vol. 5(2), item 4; Hall, p. 818.

13. LP, vol. 10, item 141.

14. CSP, Spain vol. 5(2), item 9.

15. LP, vol. 10, item 199.

16. LP, vol. 10, items 200, 427.

17. LP, vol. 10, item 284.

18. LP, vol. 10, item 282; Ives, p. 296.

19. LP, vol. 10, item 282.

20. Wriothesley, p. 43; LP, vol. 10, item 901.

21. LP. vol. 10, item 199.

22. LP vol. 10, item 495.

23. LP, vol. 10, item 601.

24. LP, vol. 10, item 752.

25. Susannah Lipscomb gives a concise overview of the varying interpretations, including those by G. W. Bernard, Eric Ives, John Schofield, and Greg Walker cited in the bibliography here. I have largely followed Walker's view.

26. Schauer and Schauer, pp. 61, 64; LP, vol. 8, item 876.

27. LP, vol. 10, items 876(6), 908.

28. Schauer and Schauer, pp. 65, 73–74.

29. Spelman, quoted by Schauer and Schauer, p. 68.

30. LP, vol. 10, item 908.

31. Cobbett, p. 424.

32. Cobbett, p. 424.

33. LP, vol. 10, item 876.

34. LP, vol. 10, item 908.

35. Cobbett, p. 425.

36. LP, vol. 10, item 908.

37. LL, vol. 3, no. 698.

38. CSP, Spain, vol. 5(2), item 55.

39. Ives, p. 354.

40. LP, vol. 10, item 909.

41. CSP, Spain, vol. 5(2), item 55.

42. LL, vol. 3, no. 697.

43. Wriothesley, vol. 1, p. 41.

44. Norton, p. 265; Thomas, pp. 116–17.

45. Wriothesley, vol. 1, pp. 41–42.

46. Hall, p. 818; LP, vol. 10, item 911; Wriothesley, p. 42; Ives, p. 423 n.9; LL, vol. 3, no. 698; CSP, Spain, vol. 5(2), item 55.

47. LP, vol. 10, items 926; LL, vol. 3, no. 706.

48. LP, vol. 10, item 901, 908.

49. For what follows see Whitelock, pp. 83–90; Edwards, pp. 46–49, LP, vol. 11, item 7; CSP, 5(2), item 70.

9 *An Opinion Given*

1. LP, vol. 10, item 212.

2. LL, vol. 4, nos. 850(ii) (p. 109), 863, 876.

3. For what follows see Schenk, pp. 62–86; *ODNB*, 'Reginald Pole'; Pierce, MP, pp. 106–08; Mayer, *Reginald Pole*, pp. 19–21.

4. LP, vol. 9, item. 701.

5. Schenk, p. 71.

6. LP, vol. 10, item 975.

7. Schenk, p. 73.

8. Mayer, 19–21.

9. LP, vol. 13(2), no. 818(19).

10. LP, vol. 11, item 93.

11. LP, vol. 11, no. 451.

12. LP, vol. 11, no. 92.

13. Mayer, *Correspondence*, vol. 1, p. 222.

14. Loades, *Mary Tudor*, pp. 105–06.

15. Pierce, MP, pp. 108–09.

16. Pierce, MP, p. 109.

17. Madden, pp. 9, 51.

18. Loades, Henry VIII, p. 283–84.

19. LP, vol. 12(2), item 911.

20. LP, vol. 12(2), item 1060.

10 *Coming to Stripes*

1. For what follows, see Pierce, MP, pp. 113–70; Loades, *Thomas Cromwell*, pp. 147–54; LP, vol. 13(2), items 795–797, 800–805, 817–818, 820–822, 826–831, and Appendix 1.

2. LP, vol. 7, no. 32.

3. CSP, Spain, vol. 5(1), item 109.

4. LL, vol. 5, items. 1259. For Morisyne, see Pierce, MP, p. 216 n.85.

5. LP, vol. 13(2), item 835 (ellipses in original).

6. Ellis, *Original Letters*, second series, pp. 110–13.

7. Ellis, *Original Letters*, second series, pp. 114–16.

8. LP, vol. 13(2), item 979.

9. Wriothesley, vol. 1, p. 92.

10. LP, vol. 14(1), item 37.

11. Pierce, MP, pp. 141–70; Loades, *Thomas Cromwell*, pp. 153–54; Schofield, pp. 316–19.

12. Bellamy, pp. 9–11, 31–32.

13. Ellis, *Original Letters*, first series, pp. 96–98.

14. Green, p. 92; Donelson, p. 140.

15. Cole, pp. 96–100.

16. LP, vol. 14(1), item 573.

17. *ODNB*, 'Sir Nicholas Carew'.

18. Froude, *History of England*, vol. 3, p. 387.

19. Froude, *History of England*, vol. 3, pp. 387–88.

20. LL, vol. 5, no. 1419.

21. Haile, p. 267; Mayer, *Correspondence*, vol. 1, p. 242–43.

22. LP, vol. 14(1), item 1133.

11 The Lady in the Tower

1. LP, vol. 14(2), item 554.

2. Green, p. 92; Donelson, pp. 144–45.

3. Pierce, MP, p. 173.

4. Donelson, p. 145.

5. Donelson, p. 146; LP, vol. 14(2), item 627.

6. Nicolas, pp. 146–47.

7. Hayward, Dress, p. 434; 'Clothed by the Tudors', pp. 74–75.

8. Strickland, pp. 298–99.

9. Nicolas, pp. 146–47.

10. Pierce, HP, pp. 174–77.

11. LP, vol. 16, items 868, 941.

12. LP, vol. 16, item 868.

13. CSP, Spain, vol. 6(1), 166.

14. Herbert, p. 401.

15. Lingard, p. 62.

16. Bell, pp. 26, 29.

17. Camm, p. lx.

18. Mayer, *Reginald Pole*, p. 112.

12 Restoration

1. LP, vol. 16, item 1011.

2. LP, vol. 17, item 880, fl. 43b.

3. For what follows, see Dunn.

4. Mayer, pp. 171–72.

5. Mayer, *Reginald Pole.*

6. CSP, Venice, vol. 5, items 764 & 766.

7. *ODNB*, Geoffrey Pole.

8. Mayer, *Correspondence*, vol. 2 no. 720.

9. Calendar of State Papers, Spain, 9 Sept. 1553.

10. *ODNB*, Edward Courtenay.

11. Cross, p. 15; CPR, 1553–54, pp. 147, 186.

12. Routledge, p. 528.

13. Cross, p. 16.

14. CSP, Spain, vol. 13, item 127.

15. Mayer, *Correspondence*, vol. 2, item 998.

16. CSP, Spain, vol. 13, item 127.

17. CSP, Spain, vol. 13, item 111.

18. CSP, Spain, vol. 13, item 115.

19. CSP, Spain, vol. 13, item 127.

20. Nichols, *Chronicle of Queen Jane*, p. 164–65. The third person was Stephen Gardiner, Bishop of Winchester.

Epilogue: Pious Ends

1. CSP, Venice, vol. 6, no. 1287. Pole provided that the residue of his estate should be distributed 'in pious causes and among persons both my poor relatives and friends and familiars or my servants' (Mayer, *Correspondence*, vol. 3, item 2286, p. 568).

2. *ODNB*, 'Sir Geoffrey Pole'; Mayer, *Correspondence*, vol. 3, p. 586 n. 308; Arnold, pp. 85–86. Constance named six children in her will: Thomas, Geoffrey, Henry, Katherine Fortescue, Mary Claufolde or Cufawde, and Margaret Windsor.

3. Pierce, MP, p. 180.

4. *ODNB*, 'Reginald Pole'.

5. CSP, Venice, vol. 6, item 1286.

BIBLIOGRAPHY

Online Sources

Calendar of State Papers, Milan (British History Online)

Calendar of State Papers, Spain (British History Online)

Calendar of State Papers, Venice (British History Online)

Center for Thomas More Studies, The Trial of Thomas More (http://
thomasmorestudies.org/docs/The%20Trial%20of%20Thomas%20More.pdf)

John Foxe's *The Acts and Monuments* Online

Letters and Papers, Foreign and Domestic, Henry VIII (British History Online)

McIntosh, J. L., *From Heads of Household to Heads of State: The Preaccession
Households of Mary and Elizabeth Tudor 1516–1588* (Project Gutenberg:
Columbia University Press, 2008)

Oxford Dictionary of National Biography

Roper, William, *The Life of Sir Thomas More*, eds. Gerard B. Wegemer and
Stephen W. Smith (http://www.thomasmorestudies.org/docs/Roper.pdf)

Vergil, Polydor, *Anglica Historia* (1555 version), ed. Dana F. Sutton (The
Philological Musuem)

Victoria County History

Published Sources

Arnold, Revd F. H., 'Lordington House, Its Owners and Associates', *Sussex
Archaeological Collections*, 21 (1869), pp. 73–89.

Arthurson, Ian, *The Perkin Warbeck Conspiracy 1491–1499* (Stroud: Alan
Sutton Publishing Limited, 1994).

Beccadelli, Ludovico, *The Life of Cardinal Reginald Pole*, trans. Benjamin Pye
(London: C. Bathhurst, 1766).

Bell, Doyne C., *Notices of the Historic Persons Buried in the Chapel of St. Peter ad Vincula in the Tower of London* (London: John Murray, 1877).

Bellamy, John, *The Tudor Law of Treason: An Introduction* (London: Routledge & Kegan Paul, 1979).

Bennett, Michael, *Lambert Simnel and the Battle of Stoke* (New York: St Martin's Press, 1987).

Bernard, G. W., 'The Fall of Anne Boleyn', *English Historical Review* (July 1991), pp. 584–610.

Bernard, G. W., *The King's Reformation: Henry VIII and the Remaking of the English Church* (New Haven and London: Yale University Press, 2005).

Bernard, G. W., 'The Rise of Sir William Compton, Early Tudor Courtier', *English Historical Review*, 1981, pp. 754–77.

Brears, Peter, *All the King's Cooks: The Tudor Kitchens of King Henry VIII at Hampton Court Palace* (London: Souvenir Press Limited, 2011).

Byrne, Muriel St Clare, *The Lisle Letters* (Chicago and London: University of Chicago Press, 1981).

Calendar of the Patent Rolls.

Campbell, William (ed.), *Materials for a History of the Reign of Henry VII* (London: Longman and Co., 1873).

Cavell, Emma (ed.), *The Heralds' Memoir 1486–1490: Court Ceremony, Royal Progress and Rebellion.* (Richard III and Yorkist History Trust, 2009).

Cavendish, George, *The Life and Death of Cardinal Wolsey* (Boston and New York: Houghton Mifflin and Company, 1905).

Chrimes, S. B., *Henry VII* (New Haven: Yale University Press, 1999).

Cobbett's *Complete Collection of State Trials*, vol. 1 (London: R. Bagshaw, 1809).

Cole, Henry, *King Henry the Eighth's Scheme of Bishoprics* (London, Charles Knight & Co., 1838).

Cooper, William Durrant, 'Pedigree of the Lewknor Family', *Sussex Archaeological Collections*, 3, pp. 89–92.

Cross, Claire, *The Puritan Earl: The Life of Henry Hastings, Third Earl of Huntingdon 1536–1595* (London and New York: Macmillan and St Martin's Press, 1966).

Derett, J. Duncan M., 'The Trial of Sir Thomas More', *English Historical Review*, July 1964, pp. 449–77.

Dodds, Madeleine Hope & Ruth Dodds, *The Pilgrimage of Grace 1536–1537 and the Exeter Conspiracy 1538* (Cambridge University Press, 1915).

Donelson, Sarah Elizabeth, 'By No Ordinary Process: Treason, Gender, and Politics Under Henry VIII' (unpublished Ph.D. dissertation, Oxford, Ohio: Miami University, 2012).

Dugdale, William, *Monasticon Anglicanum*, vol. 2, ed. John Caley et al. (London: Longman, 1819)

Dunn, Christopher Allan, 'Not by Faith Alone: Vittoria Colonna, Michelangelo and Reginald Pole and the Evangelical Movement in Sixteenth Century Italy' (unpublished M.A. thesis, Washington, D.C.: Georgetown University, 2014).

Edwards, John, *Mary I: England's Catholic Queen* (New Haven and London: Yale University Press, 2011).

Ellis, Henry (ed.), *Original Letters Illustrative of English History* (first series) (London: Harding, Triphook, and Lepard, 1824).

Ellis, Henry (ed.), *Original Letters Illustrative of English History* (second series) (London: Harding and Lepard, 1827).

Fletcher, Stella, *Cardinal Wolsey: A Life in Renaissance Europe* (London: Continuum, 2009).

Froude, James Anthony, *The Divorce of Catherine of Aragon: The Story as Told by the Imperial Ambassadors Resident at the Court of Henry VIII* (London: Longmans, Green and Co.: 1897).

Froude, James Anthony, *History of England from the Fall of Wolsey to the Death of Elizabeth*, vol. 3. (London: John W. Parker and Son, 1858).

Gairdner, James (ed.), *Letters and Papers Illustrative of the Reigns of Richard III and Henry VIII* (London: Longman, Green, Longman & Roberts, 1861).

Gee and Harvey, *Documents Illustrative of English Church History*

Goodall, John, *The English Castle: 1066-1650* (New Haven: Yale University Press, 2011).

Green, Mary Anne Everett, *Letters of Royal and Illustrious Ladies of Great Britain* (London: Henry Colburn, 1846).

Haile, Martin, *Life of Reginald Pole* (London: Sir Isaac Pitman and Sons, Ltd., 1910).

Hall, Edward, *Union of the Two Illustre Families of Lancaster and York*, ed. H. Ellis (London: J. Johnson et al., 1809).

Hall, Richard, *The Life and Death of the Renowned John Fisher* (London).

Harris, Barbara J., *Edward Stafford: Third Duke of Buckingham, 1478-1521* (Stanford: Stanford University Press, 1986).

Harris, Barbara J., *English Aristocratic Women 1450-1550: Marriage and Family, Property and Careers* (Oxford: Oxford University Press, 2002).

Hayward, Maria, 'Clothed by the Tudors: Yorkist Prisoners in the Tower 1485-1547' in Hannes Kleineke and Christian Steer (eds), *The Yorkist Age* (Donnington: Shaun Tyas, 2013), pp. 64–80.

Hayward, Maria, *Dress at the Court of Henry VIII* (Leeds: Maney, 2007).

Herbert, Edward, *The Life and Reigne of King Henry the Eighth* (London, 1741).

Hicks, Michael, *False, Fleeting, Perjur'd Clarence: George, Duke of Clarence 1440–78* (Bangor: Headstart History, 1992).

Historical Manuscript Commission, Seventh Report (London: Eyre and Spottiswoode, 1879).

Houlebrooke, Ralph, 'Prince Arthur's Funeral' in Steven Gunn and Linda Monckton (eds), *Arthur Tudor, Prince of Wales* (Woodbridge: The Boydell Press, 2009), pp. 64–76.

Ives, Eric, *The Life and Death of Anne Boleyn* (Oxford: Blackwell Publishing, 2003).

Jones, Michael K. and Malcolm Underwood, *The King's Mother: Lady Margaret Beaufort, Countess of Richmond and Derby* (Cambridge: Cambridge University Press, 1992).

Kelly, Henry Ansgar, *The Matrimonial Trials of Henry VIII* (Eugene, Oregon: Wipf and Stock, 2004).

Kelly, Henry Ansgar, Karlin, Louis W. and Gerald B. Wegemer, *Thomas More's Trial by Jury* (Woodbridge: Boydell Press, 2011).

Kingsford, C. L., 'On some London Houses of the Early Tudor Period', *Archaeologia*, January 1921, pp. 17–54.

Kipling, Gordon (ed.), *The Receyt of the Ladie Kateryne* (Oxford: Early English Text Society by the Oxford University Press, 1990).

Lander, J. R., *Crown and Nobility 1450–1509* (Montreal: McGill-Queen's University Press, 1976).

Lingard, John, *The History of England*, vol. 5 (Dublin: James Duffy and Sons, 1874).

Lipscomb, Suzanne, *1536: The Year that Changed Henry VIII* (Oxford: Lion Hudson, 2009).

Loades, David, *Henry VIII* (Stroud: Amberley Publishing, 2011).

Loades, David, *Mary Tudor: A Life* (Oxford: Blackwell Publishing, 1994).

Loades, David, *Thomas Cromwell* (Stroud: Amberley Publishing, 2014).

Loades, David, *The Tudor Court* (Totowa, N.J.: Barnes and Noble Books, 1987).

Longcroft, Charles John, *A Topological Account of the Hundred of Bosmere* (London: John Russell Smith, 1857).

Madden, Frederic, *Privy Purse Expenses of the Princess* Mary (London: William Pickering, 1831).

Mancini, Dominic, *The Usurpation of Richard III*, ed. C. A. J. Armstrong (Oxford, 1969).

Marius, Richard, *Thomas More* (New York: Alfred A. Knopf, 1984).

Mayer, Thomas F., 'A Fate Worse Than Death: Reginald Pole and the Parisian Theologians', *English Historical Review* (1988), pp. 870–91.

Mayer, Thomas F., *Reginald Pole, Prince and Prophet* (Cambridge: Cambridge University Press, 2000).

Bibliography

Mayer, Thomas F., ed., *The Correspondence of Reginald Pole* (Aldershot: Ashgate Publishing., 2002).

McIntosh, Jeri I., 'A Culture of Reverence: Princess Mary's Household 1525–27' in Alice Hunt and Anna Whitelock (eds), *Tudor Queenship* (New York: Palgrave Macmillan, 2010), pp. 113–26.

Miller, Helen, *Henry VIII and the English Nobility* (Oxford: Basil Blackwell, 1989).

More, Sir Thomas, *The History of King Richard III and Selections from the English and Latin Poems*, ed. R. S. Sylvester (New Haven and London: Yale University Press, 1963).

Morgan-Guy, John, 'Arthur, Harri Tudor and the Iconography of Loyalty in Wales' in Steven Gunn and Linda Monckton (eds), *Arthur Tudor, Prince of Wales* (Woodbridge: The Boydell Press, 2009), pp. 54–55.

Nichols, J. G. (ed.), *The Chronicle of Queen Jane and Two Years of Queen Mary, and Especially of the Rebellion of Sir Thomas Wyatt* (London: Camden Society, 1850).

Nichols, J. G. (ed.), *Collectanea Topographica et Genealogica* (London: John Bowyer Nichols and Son, 1834).

Nicolas, Harris, *Proceedings and Ordinances of the Privy Council of England, 32 Henry VIII to 33 Henry VIII*, vol. 7 (London: 1837).

Norton, Elizabeth, *Anne Boleyn in Her Own Words and the Words of Those Who Knew Her* (Stroud: Amberley, 2011).

Perkins, Thomas, *Wimborne Minster and Christchurch Priory: A Short History of Their Foundation and a Description of Their Buildings* (London: George Bell and Sons, 1899).

Philips, Thomas, *The History of the Life of Reginald Pole*, vol. I (London: 1767).

Pierce, Hazel, 'The Life, Career and Political Significance of Margaret Pole, Countess of Salisbury, 1473–1541 (unpublished Ph.D. dissertation, Bangor: University of Wales, 1997).

Pierce, Hazel, *Margaret Pole, Countess of Salisbury 1473–1541: Loyalty, Lineage and Leadership* (Cardiff: University of Wales Press, 2009).

Pierce, Hazel, 'The King's Cousin: The Life, Career and Welsh Connection of Sir Richard Pole, 1458–1504', *Welsh History Review*, 1998, pp. 187–225.

Pollard, A. F. (ed.), *The Reign of Henry VII from Contemporary Sources*, vol. I (London: Longmans, Green and Co., 1913).

Pollnitz, Aysha, 'Christian Women or Sovereign Queens? The Schooling of Mary and Elizabeth' in Alice Hunt and Anna Whitelock (eds), *Tudor Queenship* (New York: Palgrave Macmillan, 2010), pp. 127–42.

Porter, Linda, *The First Queen of England: The Myth of 'Bloody Mary'* (New York: St Martin's Press, 2007).

Powell, Sue, 'Margaret Pole and Syon Abbey', *Historical Research*, November 2005, pp. 563–67.

Powell, Edgar (ed.), *Travels and Life of Sir Thomas Hoby* (London, 1902).

Pronay, Nicholas and John Cox (eds), *The Crowland Chronicle Continuations, 1459–1486* (London: Alan Sutton Publishing, 1986).

Rex, Richard, *Henry VIII* (Stroud: Amberley, 2009).

Richardson, Glenn, *The Field of Cloth of Gold* (New Haven and London: Yale University Press, 2013).

Rous, John, *The Rous Roll* (Gloucester: Alan Sutton Publishing Ltd, 1980).

Routledge, F. J., 'Six Letters of Cardinal Pole to the Countess of Huntingdon', *English Historical Review*, July 1913, pp. 527–31.

Scarisbrick, J. J., *Henry VIII* (Berkeley and Los Angeles: University of California Press, 1970).

Schauer, Margery S. and Frederick Schauer, 'Law as the Engine of State: The Trial of Anne Boleyn', *William and Mary Law Review* (1980), pp. 49–84.

Schenk, W., *Reginald Pole: Cardinal of England* (London: Longmans, Green and Co, 1950).

Schofield, John, *The Rise and Fall of Thomas Cromwell: Henry VIII's Most Faithful Servant* (Stroud: The History Press, 2011).

Sneyd, Charlotte Augusta, trans., *A Relation, or Rather a True Account, of the Island of England* (London: John Bowyer Nichols and Son, 1847).

Society of Antiquaries, *Collection of Ordinances and Regulations for the Government of the Royal Household* (London: John Nichols, 1790).

Southworth, John, *Fools and Jesters at the English Court* (Stroud: Sutton Publishing, 2003).

Spedding, Alison J., 'At the King's Pleasure: The Testament of Cecily Neville', *Midland History*, Autumn 2010, pp. 256–72.

Stapleton, Thomas, *The Life and Illustrious Martyrdom of Sir Thomas More* (trans. Phiip E. Hallett) (London: Burns Oates & Washbourne Ltd, 1928).

Starkey, David, *Henry: Virtuous Prince* (London: Harper Press, 2008).

The Statutes of the Realm (London: Dawsons of Pall Mall, 1963).

Strickland, Agnes, *Lives of the Queens of England*, vol. 4 (Philadelphia: Lea and Blanchard, 1850).

Sutton, Anne F. and P. W. Hammond (eds), *The Coronation of Richard III: The Extant Documents* (Gloucester: Alan Sutton, 1983).

Sutton, Anne F. and Livia Visser-Fuchs, 'The Children in the Care of Richard III', *The Ricardian*, 2014, pp. 31–62.

Thomas, William, *The Pilgrim: A Dialogue of the Life and Actions of King Henry the Eighth*, ed. J. A. Froude (London: Parker, Son, and Bourn: 1861).

Tremlett, Giles, *Catherine of Aragon: The Spanish Queen of Henry VIII* (New York: Walker & Company, 2010).

Walker, Greg, 'Rethinking the Fall of Anne Boleyn', *Historical Journal* (March 2002), pp. 1–29.

Werham, R. B., *Before the Armada: The Emergence of the English Nation, 1485–1588* (New York: Harcourt, Brace & World, Inc., 1966).

Whitelock, Anna, *Mary Tudor: Princess, Bastard, Queen* (New York: Random House, 2009).

Williams, Patrick, *Katherine of Aragon: The Tragic Story of Henry VIII's First Unfortunate Wife* (Stroud: Amberley Publishing, 2013).

Wright, Thomas, *The History and Topography of the County of Essex* (London: George Virtue, 1836).

Wriothsley, Charles, *A Chronicle of England During the Reigns of the Tudors*, ed. William Douglas Hamilton (London: J. B. Nichols and Sons, 1877).

CD-ROM Materials

Given-Wilson, C., et al. (eds), *The Parliament Rolls of Medieval England* (Scholarly Digital Editions, 2005).

LIST OF ILLUSTRATIONS

1. Genealogical illustration from the Beauchamp Pageant. (British Library, London, UK/Bridgeman Images)
2. Drawing of Margaret and her brother based on illustration in the Rous Roll. (© National Portrait Gallery, London)
3. Remains of Farleigh Hungerford Castle, birthplace of Margaret. (Photo by nicksarebi)
4. Interior of Tewkesbury Abbey. (Photo by David Merrett)
5. Painting thought to be of Margaret, Countess of Salisbury. (© National Portrait Gallery, London)
6. Reginald Pole. (Hardwick Hall, Derbyshire, UK/National Trust Photographic Library/Bridgeman Images)
7. Surviving tower of Warblington Castle, built to Margaret's specifications. (Photo by Geni)
8. Margaret's chapel, Priory Church, Christchurch, Hampshire. Engraving by Charles A. Cox. (© Look and Learn/Illustrated Papers Collection/Bridgeman Images)
9. Three Roman Catholic martyrs executed on the orders of Henry VIII. (Universal History Archive/UIG/Bridgeman Images)
10. Church of St Mary, Stoughton, West Sussex. (Photo by Charlesdrawkew)
11. Effigies of Catherine Pole, Countess of Huntingdon, and her husband Francis Hastings, Earl of Huntingdon. (Photo by Andrewrabbott)
12. Henry Hastings, Earl of Huntingdon. (Anglesey Abbey, Cambridgeshire, UK/National Trust Photographic Library/Bridgeman Images)
13. George, Duke of Clarence, in the Rous Roll. (Courtesy of the British Library)
14. Elizabeth Woodville. (Courtesy of Ripon Cathedral)
15. Edward IV. (Courtesy of the Amberley Archive)

INDEX

208

Tudor History from Amberley Publishing

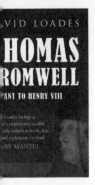 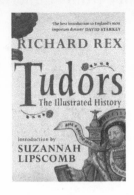 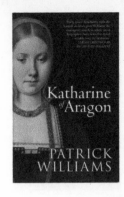

HOMAS CROMWELL
id Loades
sh, fair, lucid and a pleasure to read' *HILARY MANTEL*
9   978-1-4456-4001-3   368 pages PB   27 col illus

DORS: THE ILLUSTRATED HISTORY
ard Rex
: best introduction to England's most important dynasty' *DAVID STARKEY*
   978-1-4456-4371-7   256 pages HB   200 col illus

THARINE OF ARAGON
ick Williams
ty years' familiarity with the Spanish archive gives Williams the courage to march in where most biographers
: feared to tread – notably in the bedroom' *SARAH GRISTWOOD, BBC HISTORY MAGAZINE*
9   978-1-4456-3592-7   512 pages PB   40 col illus

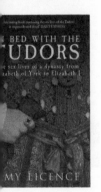 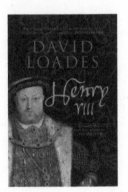 

BED WITH THE TUDORS
y Licence
plores what really went on in Henry VIII's bedroom … a fascinating book' *THE DAILY EXPRESS*
9   978-1-4456-1475-5   272 pages PB   30 illus, 20 col

NRY VIII
id Loades
vid Loades' Tudor bio   graphies are both highly enjoyable and instructive, the perfect combination'
TONIA FRASER
99   978-1-4456-0704-7   512 pages PB   113 illus, 49 col

THERINE PARR
abeth Norton
rton cuts an admirably clear path through tangled Tudor intrigues' *JENNY UGLOW*
9   978-1-4456-0383-4   312 pages PB   49 illus, 30 col

Available from all good bookshops or to order direct
Please call 01453-847-800 or go to www.amberley-books.com

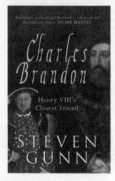
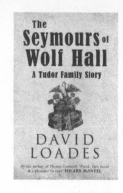

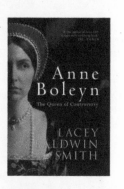
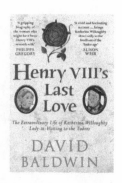